Skin, Hair & Nail Care

for Teens and Young Adults

Jennifer Leigh Youngs

co-author of the *Taste Berries for Teens* series and the *Taste Berries for Teens* Journal

BURRES BOOKS is an imprint of Bettie Youngs Book Publishers: www.BettieYoungsBooks.com

If you are unable to order this book from your local bookseller, or online from *Amazon* or *Barnes & Noble*, or from Wholesaler *Baker & Taylor*, or from *Espresso*, or *Read How You Want*, you may order directly from the publisher: Sales@BettieYoungs.com.

ISBN trade paper: 978-1-940784-44-1

ISBN ebook: 978-1-940784-45-8

Library of Congress Catalogue Control Number: 2014958418

1. Adolescence. 2. Skin Care. 3. Hair Care. 4. Nail Care. 5. Self-Esteem. 6. Appearance, Personal. 7. Body Image. 8. Self-Confidence. 9. Health. 10. Adolescent Issues.

Also by Jennifer Leigh Youngs:

- Confidence & Self-Esteem for Teens
- Health & Fitness for Teens
- Clothes, Colors and Accessories that Look BEST on YOU: A Guide for Young Adults
- Skin, Hair & Nail Care for Teens and Young Adults
- Taste Berries for Teens: Inspirational Short Stories and Encouragment on Life, Love, Friendship and Tough Issues
- Taste Berries for Teens Journal: My Thoughts on Life, Love and Making a Difference
- More Taste Berries for Teens: A Second Collection of Inspirational Stories and Encouragement on Life, Love, Friendship and Tough Issues
- Taste Berries for Teens #3: Inspirational Stories and Encouragement on Life, Love, Friends and the Face in the Mirror
- Taste Berries for Teens #4: Short Stories and Encouragement on Being Cool, Caring and Courageous
- A Taste Berry Teen's Guide to Setting & Achieving Goals
- A Taste Berry Teen's Guide to Managing the Stress and Pressures of Life
- 12 Months of Faith: A Devotional Journal for

Teens

- 365 Days of Taste-Berry Inspiration for Teens
- A Teen's Guide to Christian Living
- A Teen's Guide to Living Drug-Free
- Moments and Milestones Pregnancy Journal
- 7 Ways a Baby Will Change Your Life

Contents

Chapter One

How to Have Healthy and Beautiful Skin

Beauty is truth, and truth, beauty.
—John Keats

You are standing with friends outside of a movie theater, waiting your turn in line to go in. A girl about your own age comes walking toward you to join a friend of hers who is already in line. What is the first thing you notice about the girl approaching: The style of the outfit she is wearing? Her shoes? Her smile? The color of her hair? Her jewelry? How physically fit she is? Her demeanor?

Probably it's a combination of these things but chances are, after an initial overall glance, you focus on her face. You notice the shape of her nose and mouth and maybe the color of her eyes, but even more so than the appeal of her facial features, you specifically notice her complexion. Incredible, isn't it, that the quality of what is "skin deep" can speak so loudly as a first impression. Yet it often does.

Heirlooms: Did you Inherit Your Complexion?

Everyone compliments my mother on her beautiful complexion. She always replies by saying, "Thank you. I inherited it from my mother, and she inherited hers from her mother." There's no question that heredity can have a lot to do with the nature and appearance of your skin. A good friend of mine, Evan (who is sixteen), has a very serious case of acne—just like his father had when he was a teen. "Runs in the family," he says whenever someone reminds him of the remains of the lotion he applies to his face to heal his acne. I've met Evan's father. Judging from the deep scars on his father's face (the result of a serious case of acne he had in adolescence), it's easy to see where Evan inherited his skin condition.

But beautiful skin is more than good or back luck. Good genes are not enough to ensure that your skin will stay healthy just because you've been born with a great potential for smooth skin. And just as Mom or Dad had troubled skin doesn't mean you have to be stuck with complexion problems.

You need to take care of your skin. It begins by proper care and grooming.

Skin 101: What You Should Know About Your Skin

Understanding your skin can be valuable information. Here's a quick overview on how and why your skin is what it is, and does what it does. Your facial skin is several layers deep. The outermost layer of skin is called the *epidermis*. The epidermis is made up of two layers, a "dead-cell" and a "live-cell" layer.

As gross as it sounds, the "dead-cell" layer is what you see when you look at someone. It has an important role to fulfill: because it comes into direct contract with the external environment, this layer is our first line of defense in doing things like making the skin waterproof. It also shields the delicate "infant" cells at work growing beneath it. This layer contains cells called *keratinocytes* which vary in thickness depending on their location. For example, the skin around the eye area is only about as thick as sheet of fine paper, while that covering our heels may be as thick as a piece of leather. You are constantly shedding this layer of dead cells. These cells fall off when you shower or rub your skin with your hands or a washcloth. They slough off as you dry your face with a towel, and most especially when you exfoliate your skin (discussed later in this chapter). Pores, narrow channels that lead into a *sweat gland* or a *sebaceous gland*, are found in this layer.

The next layer of your *epidermis* is made up of living cells. These living cells divide over and over again, constantly producing new skin cells. As they do, the older cells are pushed to the surface—where they begin their function as a dead cell! This layer of living cells also contains melanocytes or pigment cells. These generate melanin, which is responsible for the color of the skin. The more *melanocytes* we are born with, the darker our skin, hair and eye color will be. In addition to being genetic, *melanocytes* can be triggered by sunlight. When you go in the sun, melanin darkens, and presto! You have a tan.

The next layer, the *dermis*, is a thick and very tough elastic layer. It contains the blood vessels bringing nutrients to the skin and carrying waste products away. Your body's nerve endings are also found in this layer, as are sweat and oil glands and hair roots. The primary purpose of a sweat gland is to aid the body in perspiring—one of the ways the body attempts to cool you down. The job of the busy little sebaceous gland is to produce oil that keeps the skin soft and flexible. It is this same gland that produces the oil to moisturize your hair and keep it healthy and shiny. The health of this layer is immensely important to the vitality—beauty—of the outer layer of skin. The effects of inadequate nutrition, exercise, rest and relaxation, as well as the effects of smoking, take their biggest toll here.

Next comes the *subcutaneous* layer, which is composed primarily of fat. Like the other layers, it's important and vital to our health and beauty. Among its many roles, this layer acts as a cushion to absorb shock (such if you were to fall down or get hit), thereby protecting the inner organs from being traumatized. And, of course, it is this fat that helps give our face and body form, and, generally, lies at the heart of a comment such as, "She's too thin."

These important layers are charged with the same things to do throughout our lives. However, during adolescence, the oil glands in the skin begin to produce more oils than they normally do, which is the biggest reason adolescence is a time when acne and other skin disorders are most common. And this is why you must care for your skin and do those things that keep it at its best. Dead skin cells, grime, makeup and perspiration can block a pore from breathing. When this happens, a plug forms that blocks a pore and thus causes pimples—blackheads and whiteheads.

When you think about all the skin does, it's really quite miraculous. You can best help it be beautiful by understanding the job it has to do, and by doing your part to keep it healthy.

The drawing below shows the skin's basic makeup and its duties:

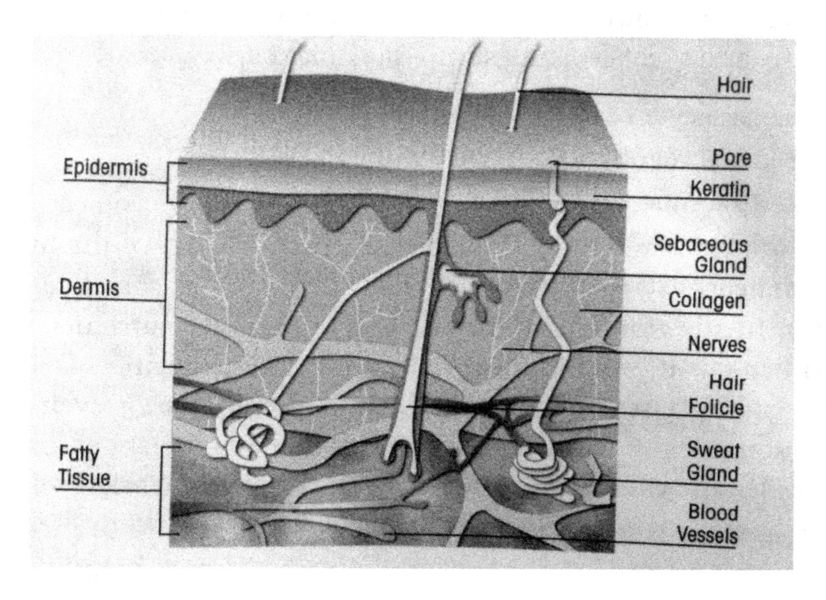

Getting the Glow: The Essentials of a Beautiful Complexion

The expression that "beauty begins on the inside" is especially true when it comes to your complexion. Drinking plenty of water, eating a healthy diet, getting enough rest, and exercising regularly are essential to the health and appearance of your skin. This may sound like the "same old, same old" advice you heard from your parents as a youngster, but as a teenager, nothing could be more important than to put into practice these commonsense yet vital basics. As every skin-care expert will tell you, "If you take care of the inside, it will take care of you." Some things, it seems, never change.

Later on in this chapter, I'll give you more detailed information on how to properly care for your skin so that you can look your best, especially through the hormonal ups and downs of adolescence. For now, here are the basic beauty treatments to have healthy and great-looking skin—sans makeup!

Beauty Treatment #1: Water It!

Drinking plenty of water is one of the best things you can do to have a nice complexion. Water is an essential part of the human body (nearly 80-plus percent in fact). Like air, we can't live without it. In addition to helping the body distribute nutrients, water also helps your system flush out toxins and impurities. Drink at least eight glasses of water a day. After doing this for even three to four days, you will notice a big difference in the appearance of your skin. It will look healthier; at the very least, it will look well rested.

Teens often ask me if soft drinks, teas and coffee can be counted in their eight glasses of daily liquids. Sorry, but nothing is a substitute for the pure water your body needs daily. In fact, drinking fluids that contain caffeine, like sodas and coffee, actually dehydrates your body. This is why doctors recommend that for every eight ounces of these types of beverages you consume, you need to drink an additional twenty-four ounces of water.

Here's a tip: If you find that drinking water is "boring," as most teens tell me it is, and your taste buds need a little encouragement to down the eight glasses of water your body needs on a daily basis, try adding a flavor (such as a squeeze of orange or lemon juice) to give a little pizzazz to the water.

Beauty Treatment # 2: Feed It!

Your diet and nutrition play a very important role not only in keeping your skin healthy but in giving it a clean and smooth and "glowing" appearance as well. Your skin is a living, breathing organ (it's the body's *largest* organ); it needs nourishment. In addition to adequate nutrients, it needs essential vitamins, minerals, amino acids and enzymes to function properly.

Feed your body foods that keep it healthy. A diet that is deficient in certain vitamins, minerals and nutrients can upset body chemistry. If your diet consists mainly of sweets or greasy foods, for example, your skin is going to react to these things. Just as not getting enough sleep shows up in tired-looking skin, especially under the eye area, the quality of nutrients you are supplying to your body shows up in the condition of your skin. Likewise, when your diet properly nourishes your cells, your skin is more likely to radiate health.

Making sure your skin is nourished properly also means no smoking. Smoking causes your blood vessels to constrict and this reduces blood flow throughout your body. Your skin has a big job to do in keeping you healthy—and alive. Among its many functions, it keeps you properly hydrated by regulating salt and water through the sweat glands. It's your body's thermostat, cooling you down and warming you up when needed. It flushes impurities from your system through the blood vessels, oil glands, sweat glands and pores. It filters out the sun's UV rays so you don't burn up.

We may think of our skin as an aesthetically appealing wrapper for our body, protecting all those internal organs so they can do their jobs, but in reality, the skin is the body's largest and busiest organ. Always looking out for us, when a skin cell begins to tire it's sloughed off, growing a new one to take its place. But as self-sufficient as it is, your skin depends on you to do your part so it can do its important work. Your skin depends on blood flow to bring the nourishment it needs. Smoking starves your body of nutrients, water and oxygen it needs to do its many task. And, smoking dehydrates your body, leaving your skin dry and pasty looking, and speeding up facial wrinkles. Be kind to your skin: don't smoke.

Beauty Treatment # 3: Exercise It!

Better overall health is one benefit of exercising. Vibrant growing skin is other. Just as our bodies need adequate amounts of the proper nutrients to stain good health, our cells depend on oxygen to function and do their work. Physical activity is the key. Physical activity increases our circulation, carrying oxygen-rich blood to the cells so they function efficiently.

Exercise really does improve the appearance of your skin, especially your complexion. My skin is always more radiant on those days after a workout than when I go several days or even a week without working out. The equation is a simple one. More oxygen circulating throughout the body keeps the cells in better condition. Good circulation speeds up the turnover of your skin cells; this helps give you fresh, healthy cells at the surface of your skin. Healthy cells means better health, a vitality that shows up in the form of beautiful skin.

Beauty Treatment # 4: Rest It!

Is sleeping one of your favorite things to do? Most young people would say yes to that question! Good news: Getting your beauty sleep is one of the skin's most important beauty treatments. How well rested you are shows in your skin. Sleep deprivation shows up in your complexion, especially in the fragile skin around your eyes, giving you dark circles and puffiness, and making you look tired and drawn.

So how much sleep do you need? Health experts say that teens need eight to ten hours of sleep each night to support the intense stage of growth and development. Added to your body's natural need for sleep, you need even more rest to keep up with your busy schedule and all the stress and strains of being a young adult.

Beauty Treatment # 5: Keep It Clean!

Keeping your skin clean is essential to having beautiful skin: Pollutants and grime in the air, makeup, as well as your body's own production of natural oils, need to be cleansed away, especially at the end of the day. When sweat, oil or dead skin is not washed away, pores become clogged and can cause irritations, such as rashes and acne. Clogged pores can stretch your skin, making pores larger and resulting in a ruddy appearance. Cleanse your skin.

Five Steps to Kissable Skin

1. Why and How to Cleanse Your Face

Washing your face is an important part of your skin care. *How* you wash it is important to your skin's health and beauty as well, and can spell the difference between having skin that is dry and looks tired, even dirty, and having skin that looks radiant and healthy—in a word, beautiful. You know this and head to the store to get yourself a good cleanser. You approach the aisle of beauty products only to discover that it's not that simple. There are literally dozens upon dozens of products claiming to help you have beautiful and kissable skin. If working your way through the maze of all the different brand names isn't perplexing enough, then the decision of which one is best is for your skin will be: soaps, scrubs, cleansing creams, astringents, exfoliants. How do you decide which is right and best for your skin-care needs?

For starters, keep your eye on the goal. Your skin produces its own natural oils as a way to keep itself healthy. Your goal is to cleanse your skin, without removing these essential oils. Secondly, select a product that is right for your skin type; is it normal, dry, oily, or a combination of these? Keep in mind that your skin needs change over time, depending on the climate, your lifestyle and even according to your hormonal changes. And remember that expensive isn't necessarily better. Read the label; look for a cleanser that says it does what you're trying to achieve: reduce oil, add moisture, cleanse only, and so on.

There are many cleansers to choose from. Here's a quick rundown:

▶ **Bar soap** (also known as *milled* soap because of the way it is produced). It's made from tallow and vegetable fats. To jazz up this basic and simple soap, lathering agents and fragrances are generally added. If you have oily, normal, or moderately dry skin, this will probably suite your needs. A word of caution however: the skin around the eye area is thin and fragile so don't "scrub" this area.

▶ **Superfatted soaps.** As their name suggests, these soap products contain lanolin and cocoa butter that give them a high fat content. They are gentle to the skin so if you have sensitive or relatively dry skin, a product containing superfats may be right for you.

▶ **Transparent soaps.** These are much the same as superfatted soaps except that they also contain ingredients like glycerin and alcohol that makes them translucent. Because of their high fat content, if you have oily, sensitive skin, this type of soap product should work for you. However, if your skin is very dry don't use these products; the alcohol content can dry your skin even more.

▶ **Deodorant soaps.** These products blend soap with antiseptics that control bacteria and hence reduce body odor.

These products are great for bath and shower, but because they are drying to the skin, never use them on your face. While it might be easier to just use whatever bar of soap is in the shower while you are showering, these products are too harsh and can also irritate the skin, making it more prone to sunburn and wind chafing. They can even cause a rash. If you dry out your skin too much, it will flake—and that's no fun. Whenever I have a peeling nose from too much sun, or a flaking forehead because I've been overzealous in applying an astringent, I'm self-conscious. I also know I've been "mean" to my skin.

▶ **Medicated soaps.** These products boast of containing ingredients specifically aimed at combating problems like acne and eczema. Unless your dermatologist or doctor has suggested you use one, you might as well save your money. You aren't going to leave soap on your face or body; once you wash away the soap, gone too is the medicating action.

▶ **Detergent soaps.** Because these are made from petroleum products and fatty acids, they tend to be less irritating than many other categories of soaps. They are oil-based, so if you have normal, dry or sensitive skin, these should work well for you.

▶ **Organic soaps.** These feature natural ingredients like plant extracts, vitamins and minerals. Save your money. Applying these ingredients to the outside of your skin offers no benefits to your skin whatsoever. Because they are packaged in such an appealing way, they look nice on your counter top though! If you are buying them for use, read beyond the rah-rah of "added" ingredients, such as plant extracts, checking to see what else they offer in the way of cleansing.

▶ **Exfoliating soaps.** These contain grains of pumice or crushed volcanic rock or cornmeal (among other things) that chafe the skin so as to remove dead cells. Though popular products, the dermatologists I consulted agreed that such products are too abrasive and too drying to be used *daily*, especially since our bodies are in a continual state of sloughing off dead cells on their own. In addition, we slough them off ourselves as we wash with a washcloth and dry with a towel.

▶ **Scrubs.** Scrubs rely on abrasive particles that also remove dead cells, but also offer emollients to moisturize the skin. There are many of these products on the market. If you decide to use one, read the label carefully. If it is alcohol-based, it can dry your skin. If it is oil-based or water-based, it won't offer much in the way of cleansing your skin.

▶ **Masks.** Facial masks cleanse the skin by removing oil, grime and dead cells. Though masks are designed to do different things, from adding moisture to soothing tired skin, essentially they are drying and most effective if your skin type is very oily. There are two types of masks, those that wash off and those that peel off. Wash-off masks are usually made up of clay based ingredients, while peel-offs contain chemicals that dry and then are gently peeled off your face. Both tend to sap moisture from the skin as they work their magic of lifting impurities from your face, which is why it is recommended they not be used more than once a week, if that.

▶ **Astringents.** These products use ingredients such as alcohol or witch hazel to "tighten" and "refresh" your skin. Boric acid, zinc, menthol and eucalyptus are often added to give your skin a tingling sensation. It's mostly hocus-pocus. Astringents offer no cleansing and no long-term "tightening," and can cause irritation and allergic reactions for those with dry or sensitive skin. Astringents are most useful for giving appearance of smaller pores, but only for a few hours. Be aware of the trade-offs.

▶ **Cleansing creams.** These products are more of a make-up remover than a cleanser. There are oil-based products (like Ponds, which my grandma uses)—typically wiped off your face with a tissue. Water-based products (also called foams, gels, gelees) are typically rinsed off. With either one you should wash your face after using it (most especially if you have oily skin) because they leave a film on your skin that you will want to remove so it doesn't clog your pores.

So there you have it. Different products (I've profiled only the major ones!), and many brands to choose from. Again, read the label; the pretty packaging should not be your consideration, nor should you buy the same product just because your best friend uses it. Understand what you are trying to accomplish, and then once you get the product home, use it as directed. If it says to leave on for a minute and you leave it on for fifteen, there may be consequences as drying your skin more than you wish, or causing a rash.

It's a good idea to wash your hands before touching your face. Your hands touch everything: Don't transfer the germs on your hands to your face.

The best way to cleanse your face is to wash your hands first and then splash lukewarm water (or pat it) on your face. Using your hands, gently apply soap or cleanser to your face, working up a lather. Leave on for about thirty seconds (or as directed) and then rinse your face thoroughly with cool water. Gently pat your skin dry with a clean washcloth (this saves on laundry). If at all possible, avoid using your soiled bath towel on your face.

Now you're ready to apply a toner.

2. Why and How to Use a Toner

Makeup, perspiration and the grime in the air form a film on your face and slow (even stop) your body's natural oil from working its way out of the pore as it normally would. Your pores can also get clogged if you don't remove your makeup at bedtime. Your pores need to breathe. Clogged pores can cause your pores to enlarge over time. (Even using overly warm water enlarges your pores.) As you recall from the material above, astringents are generally over rated and not considered to have long-lasting results. They do, however, provide a short-term solution in reducing the appearance of large pores. Because of their ingredients, toners tend to be drying to the skin, so if you decide to use one, don't overdo.

What should you look for when buying a toner? There are a good number of brands on the market. Brand name isn't at all important. Look for a toner that doesn't contain witch-hazel, alcohol or fragrance because these ingredients are drying and can irritate your skin. This is especially true if you have thin, fair or sensitive skin, or if you spend considerable time in the sun or in dry environments, like the classroom.

Do not apply toner to your entire face. If your skin is both oily and dry, use a cotton ball to apply toner to your chin, nose and forehead only. Known as the "T-zone," these are the areas with the most oil glands.

Don't rinse your toner off. It's okay to apply makeup over it.

3. Why and How to Use a Moisturizer

Do teens need to use a moisturizer to replace lost moisture and avoid dry skin? There are two schools of thought here—no, and yes. Professionals are really divided on what they think is best for teen skin. Some dermatologists are adamantly opposed, while some say it's an okay idea but an unnecessary one. Still others agree with other skin care specialists such as a Facialist and say it is an absolute must.

First the argument against teens using a moisturizer: The skin derives its moisture from our sebaceous glands. Arguably, most teens have fairly active sebaceous glands and so their skin is adequately protected from being too dry; consequently, teens have little reason to add moisturizer.

The argument for adding moisturizer is this: Our skin going about its daily duty in caring for itself may not be sufficient to combat the wear and tear of our lifestyle in today's high-tech time. Air-conditioning, overhead lighting, more frequent exposure to hot and cold temperatures, a greater emphasis on fitness (and playing sports and spending time in chlorinated pools) and hence dehydration from perspiring—all take an extra toll on the body's natural production of oils. Therefore it's smart to use a moisturizer (and most especially if you are using a medication to combat acne). So what should you do? My advice is to know your skin and make a decision based on what you think is right. For example, when I was in high school, I constantly played sports, was always outdoors, and my skin was on the dry side. I needed to add moisture. I'm going to provide you with the scoop on moisturizers so you can decide for yourself. And, of course, if you are unsure if using a moisturizer is best for you, ask a dermatologist or skin-care specialist.

Most moisturizers are advertised as "daytime use" or "nighttime use." The difference is that a daytime moisturizer usually has a sunscreen in it and is not as creamy (so makeup will go on over it). For daytime use, you want a moisturizer with sunscreen to protect against the damaging effects of the sun to your skin. Even if you are working on a great tan, you definitely want to use a moisturizer (as well as makeup) with sunscreen protection. Most makeup brands have only SPF-5UV (ultraviolet) protection, so the moisturizer you select should have at least SPF-10 of sunscreen protection. If you don't wear makeup, select a moisturizer with a minimum SPF-15 protection—which is the minimum guideline recommended by skin-care experts. Dermatologists and other skin-care specialists agree that the very best sunscreen contain these three ingredients: avobenzone, parsol 1789 and zinc oxide (more about this later).

Moisturizer versus Emollient

Sometimes you'll see a moisturizer advertised as an emollient. The difference between a moisturizer and an emollient is this:

- ▶ Moisturizers add moisture to your skin. Some contain ingredients to heal skin conditions, such as a rash or sunburn.
- ▶ Emollients are made of oils and silicones that seal in moisture and make your skin softer.

Some moisturizers include emollients. You'll pay a little more for these, but in my opinion, they're worth it. Sealing in moisture is really preferable to simply having soft skin, especially since emollients will soften your skin, too.

How often should you use a moisturizer? It really depends on your skin. If you are trying to combat oily skin, it only stands to reason you won't want to overdo it. And besides, if you slather moisturizer on, you can actually clog your pores, creating blemishes. If your skin is very dry, you will want to use moisturizer after thoroughly cleansing your skin. If you are like me, and you spend considerable time in dry environments—like the outdoors or even dry indoor air, like the classroom—you'll need to moisturize even more. But as a rule, you'll gauge your need to moisturize your skin when it needs it. For example, if you are on the swim team and spend time in chlorinated pools, or if you've just returned from three days on the ski slopes, chances are your skin is drier than normal. And, right around the time of your menstrual cycle, your skin is extra oily, so you may not need to moisturize during this time. Be attentive to the needs of your skin.

Helpful Hints for Using Moisturizer

▶ Don't overdo. If you layer on too much moisturizer you will clog your pores, making them larger, and even causing blemishes to appear.

▶ Unless your skin is extremely dry, apply moisturizer only to the areas that are drier than the rest of your face, like around your eyes (or around your nose area if you've had a cold and have been blowing your nose so frequently that it's resulted in overly dry skin).

▶ When moisturizer is applied over damp skin, it creates a thin film that allows the skin to absorb the moisturizer.

▶ Always apply your moisturizer (as well as makeup) to your face in gentle, upward and outward strokes. This is a good habit and will serve you well all your life. Gravity, age and normal wear and tear are what cause the skin to lose its elasticity and hence eventually sag, so begin now in your teen years to treat your skin gently. Why add to the problem of your skin's eventually losing its elasticity? Believe me, you will always be grateful that you practiced prevention.

▶ Do not use a petroleum jelly or baby oil to moisturize your face. Petroleum jelly and baby oil (as well as moisturizers that have mineral oils) clog the pores, causing skin disorders such as whiteheads, blackheads or deep underground pimples. When excess oil combines with the outer layer of the skin, the pores get clogged, causing you to break out.

4. Why and How to Shed Your Skin: Exfoliation

Trees shed their leaves in the autumn. Many animals shed their coats from season to season. Likewise, our skin also sheds, sloughing off the old cells as it makes ways for the new cells. Skin experts say we shed more than a million cells every day!

Skin that is shredding is dry and looks dull. New skin is fresh and clean looking. Makeup, perspiration and daily grime from the environment can mean our skin can use some help "turning over a new leaf." It's called exfoliation. Exfoliating is a new step beyond cleansing the skin of makeup and daily grime. It's a deliberate attempt to "go for the glow!" Be careful though; over-washing your face will remove too much of the oil your skin naturally needs to be healthy. And if you scrub your skin too briskly, you will over stimulate your skin.

I use a "Buff-puff" (a small sponge especially designed to gently scrub the face) every other day in my regime of cleansing my face. The important thing is to massage ever so lightly, and in circular motions. Again, facial skin is fragile.

If you can afford it, I highly recommend that you get a facial every six to eight weeks from a skin-care expert. The price of this service will vary from salon to salon depending upon the length of the procedure (a thirty-minute facial versus a ninety-minute facial) and the types of products used, so be sure to ask before you schedule so you know what to expect). Once you find a Facialist, it's also a good idea to return to her regularly for the care and treatment of your skin. One reason for this is that she will know your skin type and know how your skin responds to different products, so if your skin changes from, say, over oily to over dry, she'll know how to best help you restore your skin. As an example, for a number of years I have been going to Karina Pawlukiewicz at Karina's European Skin Care. I like her services for several reasons: She is a real pro; her skin-care training is extensive; she is wonderfully personable; and, she always best advices me on how to keep my skin healthy and in good condition—in spite of my lifestyle. So if I'm just off the ski slopes and my skin is dry and crying from the windburn and high-altitude sunburn, Karina knows exactly how to soothe it and get it glowing again. If I've been ten days abroad touring and conducting workshops, usually the change in time zones and spending hours upon hours in airplanes mean I'm exhausted and my skin is suffering from dehydration and sleep deprivation. Once I'm home, Karina is among my first calls, because my skin needs rejuvenation as much as I do.

Get in the habit of treating yourself to a facial now, and your skin will be forever grateful. I had my first facial when I was in the ninth grade. It was a birthday gift from my mother. After that, I always looked at my allowance differently, knowing that a portion of it was going to be held in reserve for a facial whenever I could make my money stretch that far. It was money well spent. Throughout my high school years, Karina rescued my skin from breakouts (from stress or hormonal imbalance); restored it from the drying effects of having spent hours playing sports in the sun; as well as buffed and shined it to a high gloss for a special occasion like class pictures or prom night.

Care for your skin properly and it will reward you by looking healthy and radiant.

5. Why and How to Detoxify Your Skin: Facial Masks

When I was in high school, a group of us girlfriends would often have a slumber party, an overnight get-together where we would analyze the latest gossip at school, discuss who was going out with whom (or wanting to), and compare notes on the latest in fashion trends and makeup tips. We would do this while in pajamas as we were listening to music, especially the latest hits—and wearing our "faces" (facial masks). Of course, having all dipped into the contents of the same jar, we all wore the same look. We even took turns as to who was to bring "the goop" (facial mask).

This meant that Jeanne, a girl with a very oily complexion, wore the same facial mask as Marianne, a girl who was on the all-state swim team and swam two hours each and every morning—in addition to swimming twice a week in competitive swim meets and sometimes even on the weekends. Spending so much time in chlorinated pools was very drying to Marianne's face. If one of us had brought a mask designed to dry one's face, this was good news for Jeanne but not so good for Marianne. And if the "goop of the day" was for adding moisture, this would be good news for Marianne but not for Jeanne.

The rest of us, with skin somewhere in between that of Jeanne and Marianne, fared little better than either of the two of them. We had no clue that masks were manufactured to do a specific thing—like dry out or add moisture. To us, a mask was a rite of passage—something the big girls did—especially those as cool as we were! Because this was our ritual, and because we really didn't know any better, we simply took pleasure in putting on "our faces" (cucumbers on our eyes, included!).

Needless to say, this is not the way to use a facial mask. Because of our different skin types and depending on our particular skin-care needs, we would have been better served if we had each purchased our own facial masks based on the needs of our skin, and simply brought them along to our slumber parties and each worn our own. And of course, there are those who would argue that a mask is "purely girlie" and not all that beneficial to keeping teen skin healthy and glowing. How useful a particular mask is to cleansing your skin depends on the type of mask you are using and how you use it. On the fun side of things, no girl would disagree that friends who come together and apply their "faces" experience a very special bonding. With our "faces in place," all "pecking order" disappears!

Facial masks are designed for any number of skin-care reasons. There are masks to *detoxify* your skin, which means to draw the toxins and impurities out; masks to *add moisture* to your skin; masks to *help rid your skin* of excess oils; masks to *soothe* irritated and sunburned skin. There are masks to *deep clean* your skin and masks to cool your skin, to *pamper it*. Not all masks designed to do exactly the same thing are equal. Each can use any number of different formulas and ingredients. For these reasons, don't just buy one because it's handy, or on sale. Read the label carefully. What is it designed to do? Are you allergic to any of the typical ingredients found in masks? I found out the hard way. Several months ago, I used a mask that contained iodine and developed a mild rash. It wasn't until I used the mask a second time that I discovered I was allergic to the ingredient in the potion. Always test the formula by placing some of it on your underarms, because that area has the same type of skin as the area under your eyes. Wait twenty-hour hours before you determine whether or not it causes any reaction before actually using it on your face.

If you'd like to try a mask but are unsure what to purchase, you might talk to your mother. Does she use a mask? Does she suggest one for you? You might also ask your family doctor or a dermatologist (a medical doctor trained in the care and treatment of skin), especially if you are considering purchasing a facial mask to combat a skin condition such as acne. (Because there are different degrees of acne, always consult a dermatologist to determine what is the best way for you to care for your skin before you resort to remedies on your own.) Another way to determine if a certain kind of mask is recommended for your skin type is to ask a skin-care specialist, such as a Facialist at a respected beauty salon or a consultant at the makeup counter at a reputable department store.

Beauty Treatment # 6: Treat Problem Skin

A pimple in the middle of your face on the day of the big dance ranks right down there with getting dumped by your best friend or seeing the boy you like holding hands with someone else. Zits are the pits. Unfortunately, breaking out is a very common problem for teens because in adolescence, the oil glands in the skin begin to produce more oil than they normally do. The result is skin bumps, zits, acne.

Acne is a condition in which the oil glands become blocked, infected and swollen, resulting in whiteheads, blackheads, pusheads (pustules) or cysts. What's the difference? To understand why these unwelcome guests intrude upon us, you need to understand that it's all about fluids from the oil glands needing to escape through the pores. If fluid cannot escape the opening of the oil pores (because it is clogged with dead skin cells, perspiration, bacteria or sebum—the cells' natural lubricant—or if the pore is simply closed), a *white-head* results. Because the skin is not inflamed, usually these are not painful. A blackhead develops in much the same way, only taking its name because of its darkish coloring (derived from your own skin pigmentation) as it makes its way from the sebaceous gland to the oil pore. The blackhead, too, is usually not painful because it isn't inflamed, which is not the case for a *pus-head* or *pustule* The pustule (the medical term sounds so much better!), on the other hand, is inflamed, therefore it hurts.

Basically, a zit comes about because the cell is trying to discharge its natural oils and by-products and they can't get out. When this happens, the cell fills up with the accumulated oils and bacterial waste products, and because these cannot escape, it swells and eventually, erupts—or tries to. Sometimes these skin conditions get better with self-care and other times they will need to be treated by a dermatologist or skin-care specialist.

A dermatologist is a skin specialist, a medical professional with special training in all areas pertaining to the skin, and can help you with the most effective way to treat your problem skin. This is especially important in cases when bacteria has infected or blocked the pores, causing cysts or bolls.

The A, B, C, and D Grades of Acne

There are different degrees of acne, and dermatologists use a grading system to distinguish between mild, moderate and severe cases.

Grade A is a mild outbreak of whiteheads and blackheads. Typically these are not inflamed and the best way to treat them is through proper cleansing. You can also buy an over-the-counter cleansing product specifically designed for acne-prone skin. Usually these will contain one (or a combination) of these ingredients: benzoyl peroxide, alpha-hydroxy or salicyclic acid.

Grade B (very typical for teens) is a moderate case of white heads and blackheads as well as pustules or pus-heads—inflamed zits. Depending on how your skin reacts to self-treatment, you may wish to consult a skincare specialist.

Grade C is an outbreak of whiteheads, blackheads and deep-seated pastules on the face, neck, chest and shoulders. You will definitely want to seek medical attention to treat this skin condition.

Grade D, just like the D in school, requires your utmost attention—and the care of a dermatologist. These deeply embedded cysts are very painful and can cause permanent scaring if left untreated.

Caring for Skin Problems

In caring for problem skin, here are some other things to remember.

▶ **Keep your skin clean.** The best first line of defense against blemishes is clean skin. If your skin is extra oily, wash it with a mild facial soap two or three times a day. In addition to cleansing your skin, you might ask a pharmacist at your local drugstore for help in finding the best over-the-counter skin medications. He or she may recommend products that contain agents that will kill bacteria, as well as treat mild cases of acne.

▶ **Don't overwash**. While it's important to keep your skin clean, if you wash it too much you can strip it of natural sebum (oil) and it may respond by overproducing oil, which leads to blackheads and pimples.

▶ **Treat the "T-Zone."** If your skin is exceptionally oily, use an astringent over your "T-zone" area during the day, as well as at bedtime. Remember to cleanse your face first.

▶ **Don't squeeze.** Skin-care specialists recommend that you not squeeze blackheads, so don't. But if you do, be extremely gentle. If you press too hard you can break skin tissue, and cause an infection, even scarring. Always make certain that the skin is clean. Wrap the tissue around your fingers (this prevents germs passing from your hands to the open wounds) before lightly applying pressure. Afterwards apply a light pat of an astringent (you can buy this at any drugstore). An astringent is used to kill bacteria and germs, and to gently dry the area in order to help it heal.

▶ **Take good care of your overall health.** Make it a lifestyle to eat healthy foods, and get adequate exercise and rest. Learn positive ways to manage your stress. Strive to be happy.

And remember, if you feel your breaking out is not because of your diet and cleansing routine, and that your complexion is taking a turn for the worse, ask your parents if you can see a dermatologist. At the very least, go see your school nurse. As always, talk to your mom and dad about your concerns for keeping your skin healthy.

Your Skin—And It's Monthly Moods

Many teens find that their skin is especially susceptible to breaking out about a week before their menstrual cycles. This is due to heightened hormonal activity and can generally be controlled by drinking plenty of water to flush out your system. (Don't worry that drinking a lot of water during a menstrual cycle will make you retain more water. The truth is, it will help flush out the water you are retaining.) Though I've come across some dermatologists who say there is little correlation between the foods we eat and breaking out, as a rule, most concur that it is wise to minimize greasy and fatty foods, as well as chocolates during this acne-vulnerable time. Moderate exercise will also help your circulation do its job, as well as reduce your PMS mood swings.

Beautiful Skin—All Over Your Body

The skin on your face isn't the only skin you want to beautiful. The skin on the rest of your body needs TLC, too.

(You Are Never Too Young to) Fake a Bake

Unfortunately, just as the sun gives our skin a nice glow, it can also cause great damage, making our skin to become leathery, wrinkled and discolored. And, overexposure to the sun's ultraviolet (UV) rays can cause skin cancer.

Tanning lamps also produce this damaging ultraviolet radiation. While much of the advertising coming from the tanning salons suggests there is no risk to damaging your skin, skin doctors tell me tanning beds are positively devastating to your skin in the long run. If you are trying to get an update on the safety of tanning salons in your area, check with a local dermatologist. He or she can best advice you what is best for your long-term skin health.

In general, the darker the skin, the less sensitive it is to ultraviolet radiation. So the fairer you are, the more committed you'll want to be to faithfully using a good sunscreen. But no matter if you are fair-skinned, dark-skinned or somewhere in between, dermatologists recommend using a sunscreen of at least SPF-15 UV protection. In many cases, you will need a sunblock to block solar radiation.

What's the difference? A sunscreen *filters* out the rays, while a sunblock stops all rays from penetrating your skin. When looking for one, read the label. You'll see a Sun Protection Factor (SPF) rating. This is a standard rating used to help you decide what level of protection you are seeking in order to keep from being burned by the rays of the sun. It's a system that allows you to judge for yourself what protection you need. For example, SPF-15 is a common number, meaning that if you were in the sun without any protection at all, wearing SPF-15 should allow you to stay in the sun fifteen times longer without burning. Common sense—and the strength of the sun, and the length of time you are in it—then, dictates which is the best one to wear. If you are going for an late-afternoon bike ride with your friend, an SPF-6 sunscreen may be adequate. If you are going to spend the afternoon water skiing, you may very well want to wear an SPF-30 sunscreen, or better yet, wear a sunblock.

Here are some other, important reminders in protecting your skin (and hair) from the harmful UV rays of the Sun:

▶ **Avoid taking a blast of radiation.** The sun gives off its strongest radiation at twelve noon, which means that any time between ten and two you need to protect yourself from the damaging effects of UV exposure.

▶ **Don't let the clouds rain on your (life) parade.** Don't be fooled by cloud cover; while they offer us a little protection, they don't filter out all the harmful UV rays.

▶ **Shop with the sun in mind.** If you are extremely fair—like a redheaded friend of mine—it's wise to wear more UV resistant clothing. Many sporting goods stores carry clothes that are especially designed to protect delicate skin. Woven fabrics like cotton, polyester and rayon block out UV rays better than do open weaves such as gauze, linen and cotton knits. White or light-colored clothes also do a better job of screening out rays than darker colored clothes. And, get in the habit of wearing hats, preferably wide-brimmed hats made out of tightly woven straw or other fabrics. These offer more protection than do loosely woven fabrics. Caps are always a cute look, but unfortunately, they don't always offer protection for the fragile skin on your ears, throat, and neck parts of your face.

▶ **Protect your eyes.** Invest in a great pair of sunglasses, ones that offer your eyes the protection they need from the sun. If you have dark eyes, you may need less filtering than those with light-colored or sensitive eyes. Expensive isn't necessarily better. Again, read the label. Protect your eyes.

▶ **Keep your lips kissable!** Don't forget to protect the delicate skin on your lips from the UV rays. Look for a balm (or lipstick) designed for protection from the sun.

Be good to your skin. Keep in mind that your skin doesn't have to be decades old before it succumbs to skin cancers. Protect it and it will stay healthier longer. You can have a great tan without paying the price of the harmful effects of the sun.

How to Look Like a Bahama Mama—Without Leaving Home

You don't have to bake in the sun to get a great looking tan. Whether you're hoping to achieve the look that prompt your friends to ask if you got your color sitting in the stands at your sister's afternoon soccer game, or to wonder if you went to the beach, you can get the ultimate sun-less tan—from a tube. There are some really great (sunless) formulas on the market, ones that don't leave your hands stained and won't wear off in those telltale streaks when you shower or perspire.

Usually those lotions designed to be used on the face contain different ingredients from those used on the body. Many teens like formulas that won't cause you to break out (though this feature is sure to be in most of the products trying to win over teens). Whatever brand you use, once you've determined the shade you want for below the neck, complement the shade of your body with a self-tanner or liquid bronzer for your face, or you can skip the self-tanner in favor of a sweep of bronzing powder. These days there are many on the market to select from.

Taking care of your skin shows you care about you and your good health. A word of caution: Should you notice any spots on your skin, discoloration, unusual freckles, moles, or warts, have them checked by your doctor or a dermatologist. At the very least, show them to your parents so they can decide if seeing a doctor is the right thing to do. Chances are they harmless, but prevention is the best policy—and a sign that you are serious in protecting your health and well-being.

Alligator Skin? Shedding with a Loofah Scrub

Do you sometimes feel that your skin belongs to an alligator? Just you can stimulate the shedding of old skin and replacement of new on your face, you can also exfoliate the skin on your entire body by gently scrubbing with a loofah sponge or a shower mitt while you bathe or shower. A loofah sponge is a natural sea sponge that is dried out. A shower mitt is usually made out of a ropelike fiber, though sometimes they are made out of plastic and in the shape of short bristles. I personally like the hand mitt because it's easier to use. I've tried the plastic bristles, but they're too scratchy for my skin. You can find a loofah sponge or shower mitt at almost any drugstore. They are inexpensive and last five to six months. The plastic one will last forever!

Unlike your routine of using a soft towel to pat your face following your shower or bath, dry off with a coarse towel. Briskly rub your skin. Doing so is good for circulation and helps slough off dry skin as well. Get in the habit of doing a body scrub every other time you shower. It will keep your skin looking a little pink at first, because circulation is increased. And, as a reminder, extra rubbing to the backs of your legs and buttocks is still the most effective way to minimize cellulite.

If you do this for several weeks, you'll notice that your skin has a healthy glow. This is because you are stimulating the skin to shed the dry skin and to replace it with new skin. Then, apply a moisturizing lotion or cream after you dry off.

Chapter Two

How to Have Beautiful Hands and Nails

The sky will bow to your
beauty, if you do.
—Rumi Jelaluddin

Tara Shipley

Tara Shipley, a senior-high friend of mine, is a very busy girl. Along with being a catcher on her school's softball team, Tara volunteers to coach a Little League team for her community center twice a week. Her school team meets every other day for practice, and competes against other schools every other week (sometimes on the weekend). Tara also works part-time at the local nursery where, in addition to her duties at the cash register, she helps customers box up and then carry their plants, soil and gardening supplies to their cars. Even with all these jobs that require her to use her hands, Tara has beautiful hands and nails.

Hands: How to Keep Yours Soft and Pretty

I know how hard it is to keep your hands and nails looking nice when you are as active as Tara. I love the outdoors and go horse riding as often as I can. Part of caring for my horse is the feeding and constant grooming—brushing, combing, washing and cleaning his hoofs. All these activities are very drying to my skin and take a toll on my nails, as well. Yet I need to have smooth skin and nice-looking nails in the work I do, which entails a great deal of time in front of an audience as I conduct workshops—to say nothing of the scrutiny my nails get as I do booksignings—or when my hands are being kissed by my guy!

Hands are high visibility: You raise your hand in class; you wave to people. You use your hands to punctuate your conversations and express yourself, you reach out to touch others and even to shake hands with someone whom you've just been introduced. For better or for worse, the condition your hands are in make an impression on others. Whether your hands are playing sports, taking a quiz, relaxing at the pool or being held by a special someone, the condition of your hands and nails reveals to others how much you tend to yourself.

Beautiful hands are well-groomed hands. Here's how you can keep yours looking their best:

- **Always keeps your hands clean**. From holding hands to shaking hands, from using our hands to guide us down stairwells to guiding our stroke in putting on our makeup, we touch and handle everything. Wash your hands with a soap that contains a mild disinfectant (this is to kill bacteria). You will find disinfectant hand soaps sold in most drugstores and grocery stores.

▶ **Dry your hands thoroughly.** This helps them from chapping and from drying out as well. Use a clean paper towel, washcloth or hand towel (soiled, moist towels have bacteria you really don't want back on your hands) to dry your hands.

▶ **Moisturize your hands after you wash them**. Keep a bottle of hand lotion beside the sink in the kitchen and one by the sink in your bath area. Get in the habit of dabbing on moisturizer immediately after each time you wash and dry your hands.

▶ **Stimulate circulation.** Whether applying moisturizer or watching TV, get in the habit of massaging your hands, particularly your cuticles. This gets the circulation going and is good for the skin. I keep a small tube of hand lotion in my purse for convenience so I can massage my hands when I have a little extra time, such as when I'm waiting for an appointment.

▶ **Use a moisturizer at bedtime.** If your hands are particularly dry, apply extra moisturizer and then wear lightweight gloves (or socks) on your hands overnight. You should be able to find gloves specifically made for this use in beauty-supply stores and in the beauty-supply section of most drugstores as well.

▶ **Get in the habit of wearing latex gloves,** if your family responsibilities (dishes, clean-up duty), part-time job or hobbies are such that your hands are frequently in water. This can prevent your skin from dehydrating (losing precious moisture necessary to their being soft and supple); shield your skin and nails from the harsh effects of detergents, disinfectants or chemical agents being used in the water; protect your nails from breaking; and if you wear nail polish, it can help prevent it from chipping.

▶ **Learn how to manicure your nails properly**, so that not only does the appearance of your nails add appeal to your hands, but so that you care for your nails in a way that promotes their being healthy.

Letting Your Fingers Do the Talking: Caring for Your Nails

Did you ever wonder why we have fingernails and toenails in the first place? Why don't the tops of our fingers and toes simply resemble the bottom sides? The answer is simple: Our nails have a very important role in keeping us healthy and in protecting our well-being.

The portion we trim, file and polish is the *nail plate*. It is primarily made up of hardened layers of keratin (and other things, like sulfur), and its primary purpose is to protect the vast numbers of intricate nerve endings as well as the multitudes of blood vessels at work below, carrying nutrients and oxygen to the tips of our fragile fingers and toes. The portion of the nail plate we see is made of nonliving cells. The nail plate extends up under our skin. This portion is called the *nail matrix* and is made up of living cells. We do see a little portion of the nail matrix, however; it's the little white half-moon-shaped potion and because of its shape is called the *lunula*—a Latin word meaning half-moon. The cuticle is the dividing line between these two, and serves to prevent infection and bacteria from invading the nail matrix. The cuticle is so important to protecting the overall health of the nail that while we often trim it, we shouldn't. Most dermatologists will tell you that gently pushing the cuticle up and under is the best practice in caring for your nails. In most cases, this is also sufficient for giving a nice appearance to the nail.

How to do a Great Manicure

Manicuring our nails is not only how we keep them pretty, but healthy as well. Give yourself a manicure every eight to ten days or as often as you need to. If you can afford to have them done professionally, do so every couple of weeks—in addition to your own self-care maintenance in between. If you can't afford a manicure, and don't like to do your own nails, have a girlfriend do them—and then you can do one for her. A manicure is not only good for your nails, but makes for a great "girl session" with a best friend.

Here are some tips on how to give yourself a manicure:

1. **Start with the right tools**. The basics: Fingernail clippers; cuticle keeper (get the kind with a rounded and slightly sharp edge to push cuticles without damaging them); nail file; three-way buffer (get the kind that has extra-fine surfaces for getting nails smooth); emery board; orange sticks (these often come in a package of six or twelve and double as a cuticle pusher and polish correctors); base coat (to help polish adhere and to fill in any irregular surface of the nails; nail polish in several colors (including clear); quick-dry polish formula; polish-preserving top-coat; nail polish remover (acetone free if you can find it) cotton swabs to remove old polish; isopropyl rubbing alcohol (to sterilize your tools before and after each use).

2. **Remove old polish**. Always use a moisturizing remover, preferably, one that is acetone free, because this abrasive chemical is extremely drying and potentially damaging to the nails. Using a cotton ball dipped in remover, gently wipe from the base of the nail outward. Gently is the operative word here: If you press hard, you will bruise your nails. (If you have ever done this, you know from experience that it hurts and for

many days!) If at all possible, avoid getting remover on your fingers. You really don't want your body to absorb this harsh chemical—and it is harsh, no matter what is says on the label. Manufacturers have yet to come up with anything strong enough to melt or dissolve nail polish without using a potent chemical, so until they do, exercise cautions and use sparingly. (The moment a gentler and better-smelling nail-polish remover product is developed, buy it immediately!)

3. **File your nails with an emery board.** File in one direction, not in a back and forth motion. This will prevent your nail from chipping and splitting, which will weaken the tips of your nails, causing them to chip and break easily. Though the shape of your nails is a matter of personal preference, a square-shaped nail is less susceptible to breaking, splitting and chipping. When filing, be gentle so as not to damage your nails: The thinner your nail the finer the emery board should be. Unless your nails are very long, it's better for the nail to be filed than it is to be cut with a clipper. The reason is that this is less traumatic for the nail plate.

4. **Tend to your cuticles.** Use cuticle softener (such as moisturizer or cuticle oil), applying it to the edges of your nails and massaging it in gently. Using an orange stick (not cuticle clippers), gently push the cuticle away from view. Don't cut "in" to your cuticle because that will cause it to bleed. Clip any hang nails, but do this gently, being conservative in how much skin you remove. (If you have been trimming your cuticles or getting a professional manicure and the manicurist has been trimming them ask her to instead use an orangestick.) While cutting the cuticle is standard practice in many salons (though not all), it is not good for the health of your nails.

5. **Use a Cotton ball dipped in an astringent** (like lemon

juice, though alcohol works, too) to **remove any excess oil**. This will make your go on smoothly without bubbling.

6. **Apply a base coat**. This will make your polish stick better and will fill in any irregularities in your nail. Stroke from the base of the nail to the tip. Let this base coat dry before applying nail color.

7. **Use a one-coat polish, brushing it on in smooth**, even strokes. Look for a polish that contains both a color and a top coat. It's a great time saver, and it works better than using two separate products (though you should apply two coats if you are using standard nail polish).

8. **Correct mistakes.** If you aren't as steady-handed as you'd hoped, you can correct a mistake by dipping a cotton swab in polish remover and carefully trace the skin around the nail, rolling the swab as you go so the cotton stays clean.

9. **Add a seal coat.** If you are using an all-in-one polish, one that is both polish and top coat, then add a seal coat. This helps protect the finish and adds a high-gloss look. Stroke from the base of the nail to the tip of the nail, wrapping down under the nail. This will add a protective sealer and help prevent chips.

It's a wise idea to go without polish for two to three days before painting your nails once again. Giving your nails a break from polish not only gives your nail plate a chance to breathe and repair itself, it also gives it a break from the staining caused by adding color to your nails. (Because nails are porous, dark polish stains more than do pale or clear colors.) If your natural nails look faded or yellowish in color, one reason may be because the color of your nail polish has stained the nail plate (check to be sure you have a good base coat—which should prevent yellowing—and are applying it correctly). Another reason may be because you have an infection (yeast infections are most common from nail polish). Should you notice that the yellowed nail appears crusty or that the nail is splitting and peeling, you need to see a doctor as soon as possible.

Imitations Limitations

I was at a restaurant last week having lunch with Siena Tarkington, a good friend of mine. As we were paying for our lunches, I watched with amazement as the cashier used the eraser end of a pencil to literally tap our tab into the cash register. The woman had on nearly two-inch-long fake nails. They looked more like a bear's claw or an eagle's talons than a human's fingernails! To make matters worse, they were painted in a deep dark purple, and each one studded with a different-colored rhinestone.

As elaborately decorative as I'm sure her manicure was meant to be, it wasn't pretty. My next thought was that the plastic extensions covering her natural nails got in the way of her doing her job. It also struck me how lucky I was that this employee was at the cash register—and had not been in the kitchen preparing my food! Her nails not only looked like a disadvantage in her work, they also looked unsanitary. Keeping your hands and nails well-groomed and cared for is a part of staying healthy—and looking your personal best.

What You Should Know About Fake Nails

Personally, I don't recommend that you get fake nails for a couple of reasons. First of all, the teen years are a good time to be really active and involved in any number of activities, and artificial nails can be a hindrance to getting involved and doing these things. Take sports for example: The physical workout is a great way to keep in shape and burn off tension, as well as to help level off the oftentimes runaway emotions caused by all the hormonal ups and downs. Team sports especially can win you friends; being together, striving together, competing together builds respect and admiration for each other. The benefits are simply too good to miss out on.

The teen years are also an important time to be involved in all sorts of hobbies. After all, this is a time when you are in an active search to find your interests and talents and trying to find an interest big enough to pursue as a job, work or even as a career. Again, these years are so important—too important to miss out on—and most especially because you are having to be protective of your fake nails. When I was in high school, the girls who wore artificial nails always seemed to shy away from certain activities for fear of breaking or tearing a nail. A good friend of mine wore her artificial nails so long that she couldn't even snap a photo. I thought of her nails as a limitation to the fun the rest of us were having. The girls who went out for sports or really enmeshed in other activities, on the other hand, couldn't be bothered; they were having so having so much fun and focused on their goals. For them, artificial nails weren't worth the trade-off.

While some of the girls in my school wore fake nails because they felt artificial nails offered their own nails an added protection—because their own nails were either too weak or too brittle to withstand the lifestyle—most of the girls who wore fake nails did so because they felt artificial nails were the "in" thing to do.

Natural nails will always be in vogue. If you look closely at the hands on the models in the top magazines, you'll note that almost all of them wear short nails. Short nails that are well cared for are pretty nails. You can see my bias here. I'm making the case for wearing our own nails, and for wearing them at a length that looks nice and allows you to use your hands. This is not to say that you shouldn't apply artificial nails for those special occasions when you want your nails to be longer or more glamourous than the way you normally wear them. And this brings me to the second reason you probably don't want to wear fake nails. Your natural nails are porous, that means they need to breathe. When you cover—or rather, smother—them with a layer of plastic or acrylic, the moisture that would normally evaporate is locked in. It doesn't take too long before the nail is saturated in its on moisture. This causes it to become soft, and as a result, it loosens from the nail bed. In a word, it is a ruined nail. The nail has been destroyed. Until it grows completely out, your nail is too soft to sustain itself. As a result, it chips and peels easily.

Wearing a covering over your own natural nail for so long—glues, adhesives, acrylic, plastic—is also why fake nails are associated with some nasty infections. There are of course some alternatives. Glue-ons and tips are great short-term remedies, especially for special occasions when you want to even out a broken nail (easy to do with glue-ons or just adding a tip), wear your nails longer than you normally do (easy to do with glue-ons or just adding tips), or want to have your nails decorated in a wildly fun sort of way (easy to do with glue-ons).

Options! Decisions! Choices! How do you decide? Here's the scoop on fake nails.

The Scoop on Nails: Acrylics, Wraps, Tips, Glue-ons and More!

Whether you are just curious about artificial nails or chose to wear them because you feel your own nails are very soft or too brittle and believe that by wearing artificial nails, your own nails will have the time to "recover"—get longer, harder, stronger or whatever—the following information should prove useful in helping you make wise choices in the care of your nails.

▶ **Sculptured nails.** This process is best done in a salon. Most teens find it messy and difficult to do for themselves. The process is this: A mold is placed over your own nail (this guides the shape). Next, layers of acrylic are brushed on until the desired length and thickness is achieved. The nails are then filed and polished (if not already pre-polished). As your natural nail grows, there will be a noticeable gap between your natural nail and fake nail, so you have to return to the salon to get what is called a "refill," which is filling in, or rather, covering up of the new portion of your natural nail so as to make your fake nail.

Upside: Sculptured nails are very realistic looking.

Downside: Sculptured nails are devastating to your natural nail. Precisely because acrylics stay so long—covering and smothering your natural nail—they saturate, soften and weaken the nail plate, and often completely destroy the nail bed below. Because acrylic is highly toxic material, it can irritate the cuticle as well as the skin surrounding the nail. Acrylics are notorious for causing serious nail infections. Expect to be in the salon an hour or longer. And they are expensive, depending on the particular salon you use.

▶ **Wraps:** This is best left to a salon manicurist as well. The process is this: Strips of silk paper or linen are applied over your own natural nail and wrapped just under your own natural nail. They are then trimmed to size and glued on your nail. After this dries, the wrap is manicured like a natural nail.

Upside: These nails will last anywhere from one to three weeks.

Because your nail has been reinforced, your nails feel durable (especially if you considered your own natural nail weak).

Downside: Because they stay on so long, they can soften and weaken the nail plate. They can cause infections. They can cause short-term and permanent damage to your nail. Expect to be in the salon an hour or longer. They are expensive.

▶ **Press-on nails.** You can buy these at beauty-supply stores and in most drugstores, even grocery stores. The process is this: Select the nails that appeal to you. Within the package of nails you should find an adhesive that is meant to be applied over your own nails (follow the specific directions contained in the package you purchase). Applying one nail at a time, press the fake nail over your own. Since you buy them in the length of your choice, you shouldn't have to cut or file these artificial nails. Some brand names offer the gel-adhesive already on the nail. With these, you simply peel back the protective coating and apply the fake nail to your own. Allow the specified time to dry so that it adheres snuggly to your own nails.

Upside: These plastic nails come in a wide variety of shapes, lengths and colors so you can readily change them as you wish. Because they don't stay on long (one to four days) there is less (if any) damage to your natural nail. They rarely cause infections. They are inexpensive.

Downside: They don't look as natural as do, say, sculptured nails. They are known to pop off easily, so they aren't as dependable as some other artificial nails.

▶ **Nail tips.** These are made from acetate and can be applied at home or at a salon. The process is this: The acetate nail is selected to match the size and shape of your other nails. It is then cut and trimmed so that it matches perfectly. Then it is applied over the tips of your own nails and glued on with an acrylate adhesive. Next, a mixture of acrylic powder and glue is applied over your entire nail so that the nail tip looks like a natural extension of your own nail. Your nails are then polished in the color of your choice (even as a French manicure).

Upside: They look natural. If overall your nails are in nice shape except for a nail or two that is broken, you can have a tip put on so that it matches the length of your other nails. And of course, you can have a tip applied to each of your nails. As a rule, most salons charge $3 a tip, and often a little less depending on how many you have applied. Nail tips are easier to remove (they need to be soaked off with a special solution, though they can fall off from natural wear and tear).

Downside: Because nail tips don't really have much to hang on to—just the tip of your own finger—a very strong adhesive is used to glue them on. This adhesive is so strong that it is often associated with severe allergic reactions, especially if you put your fingers near your (sensitive) eyes.

Nail-care specialists confirm that in a great many cases, wearing artificial nails not only can cause infections, but also can damage your natural nails, even to the point where they never are as strong and healthy as they should be. You really have to ask yourself if it's worth wearing them.

Having Pretty Hands Is in Your Hands

Having beautiful hands and nails can give you added confidence in the way you present yourself, secure in knowing your hands are a spokeswoman of your good grooming—and good health! Like most things, having pretty hands is in your hands.

Chapter Three

How to be Good to Your Feet

Make time away from highways and promises, time for quiet, peace and love.

—Peter Stone

Putting Your Best Foot Forward: Facts from a (Highly Paid) Foot Model

I have a good friend, Angeline D'iamto, who is a shoe model. Sounds like a great job doesn't it, getting paid big sums of money to model the latest and hottest fashion in shoe designs! But Angeline, like the rest of us, has got to do her homework. In her case, it's making sure her feet are in top-notch condition—or she won't be selected for a job.

Caring for your feet regularly throughout the year makes all the difference in looking great as well as in your sense of comfort—no matter if your feet are making their appearance for your eyes only, or if you're wearing bare feet in dress sandals to a special someone's wedding. I asked Angeline to share her secrets for having beautiful feet. Here they are:

- ▶ Wear comfortable shoes, which means wear "flats"—shoes without heels—even to dress-up events!
- ▶ Apply Vaseline to your feet and wear socks to bed every night—even in the summer!
- ▶ Get a pedicure every ten days.
- ▶ Exfoliate your feet every other week.
- ▶ If you must wear high heels, limit the amount of time you spend standing in them.
- ▶ Never get athlete's foot!

Are you surprised at how commonsense these tips are? All of them are easy for any of us to follow.

Hazardous High Heels: Comfort Counts

When I was a sophomore, I was asked out by a guy who was a senior. He had dated a really pretty girl who always dressed nicely. Several months after they broke up, he asked me out. He was a neat guy and a popular one. I was flattered. I can't tell you how much I waited for the day of our date!

As soon as he asked me out, I got busy thinking about shopping for just the right things to wear on that first date. My goal was to look good—well actually, my goal was to look drop-dead gorgeous. And I did. From a great outfit to the most incredibly dainty, strapping three-inch sandals, I was smashing! The problem was, my toes were getting a smashing, too. Before my new love and I had even arrived at the restaurant, the little straps cut into my feet. By the time dessert was served, the hollows of my feet were burning so badly I could hardly concentrate on what my date was talking about. And I never did make it through more than one hour of dancing before I simply didn't care what he was talking about, even though he was whispering sweet nothing in my ear! I simply had to get out of those strappy little sandals before I was going to faint from the pain of them.

Do you own a pair of shoes that feel like a torture device after spending a few hours walking, dancing or even just standing in them? Most of us girls do. Think of those flashy and adorable spike heels with the pointy toes and flashy straps that looked gorgeous with your prom dress—you know the ones—you carried them out the door as you hobbled out after a couple hours of dancing in them. I've learned to wear comfortable shoes, especially these days when I'm doing workshops and seminars and am on my feet for hours at a time, and sometimes for a full day. When my feet hurt, I hurt all over. My foot-modeling friend made it perfectly clear that comfort counts for her, too. She *always* wears comfortable shoes.

Foot specialists, known as *podiatrists*, agree that wearing comfortable shoes, ones that fit well and don't have a high heel, is always the best thing you can do for your feet. Even if you adjust to the discomfort of high heels and narrow toed shoes, there's still a price to pay in the damage they can do to the health of your feet. From pain to deformities, the shoes we wear do more damage than the wear and tear we put our feet through.

My foot-model friend says she wears low heels no matter how formal the occasion. If you've got a closet filled with hazardous heels, you'll want to limit your standing time in them. If you're going to a really fancy occasion that includes dinner at a nice restaurant and a play, you might decide to go ahead and wear your heels. If you'll be dancing or doing a lot of walking, better take along a backup pair for comfort. If you'd rather be comfortable than carting along a second pair of shoes, wear a pair that can take you through the entire evening in ease. Enjoy yourself—go for comfort.

How to "Shed" the Skin on Your Feet

Rough, dry and broken skin on your feet can be anything but attractive. You've learned about exfoliating the skin on your face and your body. You can also exfoliate the skin on your feet, adding to their beauty—and to your comfort. Exfoliating the skin on your feet can prevent dry layers of skin from building up and becoming callused.

Okay, so your boyfriend is going to hold your hand, not your foot—although many a boyfriend of mine rubbed my feet as a sweet gesture, especially when at times the two of us would be watching television. There were times when I was more than happy to leave my socks on—because of the condition my toes or feet were in. And, there were other times when I was more than happy to remove my socks and let my pretty and soft feet be romanced.

How do you keep your feet smooth and soft? Like Angeline, you can wear Vaseline and socks to bed every night—even in the summer. If the skin on your feet is really dry and cracks easily, before you go to bed try massaging your feet with a moisturizing cream that has emollients and then cover them up with socks overnight. This keeps the moisture in and warms it up so that it does a deeper job of soothing and smooth your feet. Angeline uses a mixture of sugar and olive oil on her feet after showers. After smoothing this mixture onto her feet, she rinses them and then pats them dry. I tried this little secret of hers myself and found that it really did make my feet feel velvety. Try it for yourself.

Pampered with a Pedicure

A good pedicure after you've washed your feet is the epitome of being pampered, and it assures that your feet will look and feel their very best. But a pedicure, like a manicure, is also important to nail and health care. While we may not need (or be able to afford) a weekly pedicure, it's a good idea to have one every ten days to two weeks. Pedicures are expensive for most teens, but the good news is that you can do them yourself.

Here are some important tips for doing your pedicure.

Terrific Toe Tips

- Do dry off thoroughly. After bathing or showering always completely dry your feet and between each toe with a towel. This helps prevent fungal infections.

- Do get the proper pedicure tools, and do clean them with soap and water, or with anti-bacterial spray, or isopropyl rubbing alcohol before and after each pedicure.

- Immediately following a shower or bath, push back cuticles and use a pumice stone to smooth away calluses or to remove dead skin cells.

- Don't cut your nails when they are wet or damp. Wet nails are more prone to tearing.

- Don't use cuticle nippers to cut your nails or you'll end up with torn nails (and dull nippers).

- Don't cut your nails too short; short nails are more prone to becoming ingrown. It's best to cut them blunt, then file them so they are straight across.

- Do use an emery board to shape your nails (a metal file can weaken them).

▶ Never use a razor to remove calluses. Instead, see a foot specialist or your family doctor. He or she will know the best way to treat these conditions. (This is especially the case should you suffer from an ingrown nail, or should you have developed a really bad blister that becomes infected.)

Polished Pretty Policies

You can polish your toenails like a pro. Here's how:

▶ Turn the polish bottle upside down and roll it from side to side rather than shaking it, which can make bubbles in it.

▶ Sit on a chair with your knees close to your chest. Use the hand you aren't polishing with to hold the toe you are painting.

▶ Before applying polish, clean the excess from the side of the brush that you won't be using. On the side that you're using, leave the polish on half of the brush for the big toe and just on the tip for the little ones.

▶ If you are right-handed, start polishing on your left foot, from pinkie to big toe; on your right foot, from big toe to pinkie. Lefties should work from right to left.

▶ Wait two to three minutes between coats to prevent streaking. The more coats you apply, the longer each will take to dry. Painting nails before bed is not such a good idea because nail polish takes a long time to set and when your nails come in contact with the sheet, it dulls the appearance of the glossy look you were trying to achieve.

▶ Re-dip the nail-polish brush before painting each nail, so polish doesn't have time to dry on the brush and cause streaking.

▶ For a fast long-lasting pedicure, use light frosted nail colors—mistakes and chipping won't be obvious.

▶ Prolong the life of your pedicure by applying a base coat and one coat of color the first day, a second coat two days later, a top coat whenever you need to revive the shine. Using fewer coats reduces the chances of chipping.

▶ If you don't have time for polish, use a nail buffer to smooth and shine the surface of the nail, then apply a dab of nail oil.

There's a Fungus Among Us: Athlete's Foot!

As Angeline says, the worst thing that can happen to her job-wise is that she come down with a foot fungus. Athlete's foot may not be the occupational disaster for you that it is for my friend the foot model, but you certainly want to do all you can to avoid it.

Athlete's foot is a common fungal infection that causes burning, itching, cracking and peeling of the skin on the bottom of the foot and between the toes. It's definitely a "no" to having clean and beautiful feet. To prevent it, keep your feet dry and wear absorbent cotton socks. No matter how good your friend's intention in offering to loan you a pair, avoid sharing socks. Also avoid sharing washcloths and towels. Sprinkle your soles and between toes with powder in the morning to help prevent athlete's foot and other types of fungus. The bad news is that athlete's foot won't go away on its own. The good news is that there are medications that can control the infection, so if you do get it, go to a drugstore and ask the pharmacist to recommend the "latest and best cure." If you develop a severe case, by all means see a foot doctor or your family doctor.

"Toe" Your Weight!

From comfortable shoes to protecting your feet against fungus, from trimming your toenails to painting them in a pretty shade of polish, all are about head-to-toe beauty. Your care and attention to this beauty "footwork" assures you a better chance for healthy, attractive feet. As you know, healthy feet are happy feet!

Chapter Four

Simply Beautiful Hair

Nothing is so common place as to wish
to be remarkable.
—Oliver Wendell Holmes

Hair with a Reputation

A good friend of mine, Michelle Geller, has exquisitely beautiful hair. It's long, thick, lustrous and cut in a style that frames her face in a most flattering way. It's so well-kept that your eyes are just instantly drawn to it. In fact, Michelle's hair is so dazzling that she's become known by it, a point that became clear one day when one of the girls at school commented that Lane Thomas—a really cool senior at our school—had asked Michelle to the spring dance. "Who is Michelle?" one of the girls in our group inquired, only to be informed, "You know, that girl with the really beautiful hair!"

"Oh, yeah, her!" came the first girl's instant reply. While not everyone in our school knew Michelle personally, almost all of us could identify who she was at the mention of her lustrous hair.

Mane Advice: How to Have Beautiful Hair

As her friends found out, dazzling hair makes a lasting impression. In fact, beautiful hair has so much sex appeal that at first glance, we often describe someone as "attractive" by mere virtue of the overall glamour of her hair.

What makes for beautiful hair? For starters, luster, that glossy look that we associate with healthy, vibrant hair. But glossy hair is more than a by-product of being undamaged: When the outer layer of a strand of hair, the *cuticle*, has suffered no damage (from sun, blow-drying, rollers) and is naturally well-oiled, it's smooth and even. As such, it is a surface that reflects the light; it shines. On the other hand, should the surface of your hair strand be damaged—because it is not getting adequate natural oils or is overly dry—then the surface of the hair splits apart, looking dull or in poor condition. Certain shampoos and conditioners can temporarily add shine and lustre to your hair by filling in the cracks and tears to the surface of the strand, but they cannot repair your damaged hair. (Setting lotions, gels, mousses, hairsprays and dyes leave a residue on your hair that can also make it appear dull.)

Again, hair that is not damaged is beautiful hair. And of course, volume, a good cut and a style that works for your face are also essentials to a beautiful mane. Here are some very important "beauty treatments" on how you can have great hair.

Beauty Treatment #1: Groom from the Inside

Good grooming certainly plays a big role in having great hair, but perhaps more than the color, cut or style, beautiful hair's first beauty treatment begins from the inside out. Again, diet, rest, exercise and drinking plenty of water are important to being healthy. Hair follicles are nourished by the foods you eat—your diet.

As important as good grooming is, my hair is always at its "best" during those times when my diet is good and when I stick to a regime of regularly working out and getting the sleep I need. Drinking plenty of water is important, too. When I don't do these things, and when I splurge on food such as hamburgers, French fries and chocolate, not only is my hair greasy and less manageable, it lacks shine and doesn't have the vibrancy it normally does. Just as our hair is susceptible to the elements to which it is exposed, humidity for example, it is sensitive to what's going on inside. Contrary to what you read on many of the hair-care products, your hair can not be "invigorated" or "rejuvenated" from the outside.

You may put additives on your hair that will make it shine and make it appear more full (though some products, as well as exposure to the elements or even illness, can cause your hair to be overly dry and brittle and break off) but nothing will "feed" it or make it grow. All that happens from the inside out. This is because your hair is a nonliving fibrous protein (keratin). The hair root, however, is alive, and is nourished not from the outside, but rather, from the inside.

Beauty Treatment # 2: Wash It

Cleanliness is not only a first impression of your hair's beauty—but of you, too. When you see someone who doesn't keep her hair clean, do you wonder if she took a shower, or brushed her teeth, or. . . ? No doubt about it, clean hair is a real positive in your appearance.

How often should you wash your hair? It depends. Not everyone needs to wash her hair every day, particularly if your hair tends to be on the dry side and needs to be washed less frequently.

While it's important to have clean hair, you can overdo it. If you have very oily hair, you probably need to wash your hair every day. If you have normal to dry hair, you only need to wash your hair every other day, maybe even every third day. Too much washing will wash out the natural oils in your hair, oils that are needed to keep your hair strong and healthy. Then your hair is dry, looks dull and lacks luster.

You will have to monitor this for yourself based on your hair type and how often it needs shampooing to feel clean and look its best. Luckily, there are many hair-care products on the market designed with our individual needs in mind. You can find an assortment of hair-care products in most drugstores and beauty-supply stores. Should you have questions about which products are best for you or how they should be used, sales clerks at beauty supply stores are a good source of information because not only do they hear about the product from the manufacturer, they also hear what does and doesn't work from their other customers. And of course, a visit to a hair salon for a consultation with someone trained in hair care can prove useful in helping you determine your hair type as well, as well as the best ways to care for your particular hair.

Is There a "Best" Shampoo?

There are many shampoos on the market. If you compare a handful of hair-care products, you will notice that while packaging and cost vary a great deal (expensive does not always mean better), most of the products contain the same basic ingredients, but there are some differences. So read the label before you choose a product. The first rule is to choose a shampoo according to your hair type: dry, oily or normal. The bottle will say, "for dry hair," or "for moderate to oily hair." If you can't tell if your hair is oily or dry, it probably isn't either. Hair-care experts say a simple way to determine your hair type is to pluck out a single strand of hair.

Holding this strand between both hands, pull it apart. If it snaps easily, your hair is either fine or oily. If the strand is hard to break, it means your hair is either coarse or dry. If you still can't tell the difference, schedule a consultation with a hair-care specialist at a beauty salon to advise you as to the condition of your hair, as well as suggest the best way for you to care for your hair.

You may be surprised at what you find out. For example, perhaps you use spray and mousse on a daily basis and because of the sticky buildup (residue) you wash your hair every day. As a result, your hair is dry. Because your hair is dry, and because you wash it daily, you think you should use a mild, moisturizing shampoo so as not to make it any dryer than it already is. But consider that perhaps you are adding to the problem by over-washing your hair. A hair-care specialist may very well advice you to forget the mild moisturizing shampoo and instead use a stronger one so that you can wash your hair less frequently in order to give your hair and scalp the chance to rehydrate between washings. Or, if you have extremely dry hair or your hair splits easily, you may be advised to use a special conditioner as opposed to changing your shampoo.

Should your hair be damaged from products with chemicals designed to straighten or dye your hair, you may be advised that the "magic cure" is a shampoo (as in protein-enriched shampoo) versus a conditioner. Again, a professional can help you decide what is best for you, including suggesting the best comb or brushes that work best with your hair type.

And there is something else you need to consider. Just because you are in the habit of buying shampoo for, let's say, dry hair, don't assume it will always be dry. If you observe closely, there are times when your hair type changes. For example, it may be more oily during your menstrual cycle than the other twenty-five days of the month. And, depending on the season—and most especially if you live in climates where you have a hot or cold season followed by a wet season—you may need to vary your shampoo from time to time. Regardless of the seasons and changes in environments, however (and even if your hair is naturally oily), always buy hair-care products that are alcohol-free. Alcohol dries out your hair and scalp and can contribute to dandruff and other scalp problems.

With all the shampoo products on the market, it can be confusing knowing what to buy. Don't just grab that first one on the shelf, and don't just buy the one with the pretty packaging. And unless the one you've been using works just fine for you, the next time you are ready to purchase a shampoo, stop and read the label carefully. You may have to experiment with a couple of kinds of shampoo, but it's worth it. And of course, depending on your hair care needs, you may need a couple of different kinds. I use three different shampoos, depending on what condition my hair is in.

Basically, there are two types of shampoo: cleansing shampoo and conditioning shampoo. The difference is this: *Cleansing shampoos* contain additives that are designed to clean your hair, to remove hair oils and strip off the buildup left by hairsprays, mousse, gels or other hair-care products (but not *permanent dyes*). *Conditioning shampoos* have additives designed to improve the appearance of the outer structure of your hair and make it easier to style. Whereas a cleansing shampoo is pretty straightforward, you will find there are a number of additives in the conditioning shampoos, all supposedly designed to do various things. The following profile on shampoos can help you sort out what may work best and when:

▶ **Protein-enriched shampoo**. Sometimes you will see these advertised as pH-balanced. These are formulas designed to improve damaged hair. Hair-care experts say they work because they are designed to coat the damaged hair and fill in the cracks or spit ends, making the hair appear more full. And, hair that is smooth reflects the light, so this product would also make your hair have luster, shine. If your hair is badly damaged (especially if the tips are split or frayed) you may want to try a product that is protein enriched.

▶ **Moisturizing shampoo.** These products are designed to trap moisture in the hair strands, thus preventing them from drying out. If you have normally dry hair (or limp hair) or if you spend a great deal of time outside in the elements, a moisturizing shampoo might be right for you.

▶ **Balsam shampoo.** Balsam (sometimes advertised as body-building shampoo) is an additive that strengthens and thickens the hair. It does this by restoring the damaged shaft. If you have very fine or limp hair or simply want the look of fuller hair, you may want to try a conditioning shampoo with this additive.

▶ **Herbal shampoo.** These are designed to soften the hair, make it manageable and to intensify its color. Ingredients such as aloe, honey and vitamins are all promoted to be spectacular for your hair. The hair-care experts I checked with said that while ingredients such as these make the products sound wonderfully useful, they couldn't vouch for them doing what they say they will—though they do add to the expense of the product. Again, you can't feed the hair from the outside. It's an inside-out job! One additive is worth special consideration however, and that is sunscreen ingredients, such as cinnamates and PABA. We often forget that UV rays can take their toll on hair, but they do. I suggest that you always look for these additive in any hair-care product.

The best, basic advice on shampooing is this:

- If your hair is normal or normally oily, try a cleansing shampoo.

- If your hair is dry, brittle, sun damaged or dyed or bleached, try a pH-balanced shampoo.

- If your hair is limp, thin or exceptionally thin, try a body-building shampoo.

- If you have a special condition, such as dandruff, or if you have picked up a case of head lice, buy a shampoo specifically advertised to go to work on the problem you are addressing. If you are following the directions and the shampoo isn't resolving the problem, see your family doctor or dermatologist. At the very least, go see your school nurse or tell your parents. It's important to treat these conditions. Always do those things that protect your health and well-being.

Here are some other tips on washing your hair:

- Unless your hair is really oily or unless you use hairspray, spritz and other hair-care products on a daily basis, *you do not need to apply shampoo more than once* when you wash your hair.

- Since shampoo can dry out the tips of your hair, apply the shampoo mainly to the roots and the scalp.

- Hot water is drying to your hair, so avoid using very hot water when you wash it.

- Make sure you rinse your hair thoroughly after shampooing. Because of its drying effect, you want to be sure all soap is rinsed out.

- Use the coolest water you can tolerate for the final rinse. In addition to stimulating the circulation in your scalp, cool water will close the hair cuticle, which prevents the ends of your hair from looking split and frizzy.

Oily Bangs?

Don't assume that if your bangs are oily it means that the rest of your hair needs washing. If you wear bangs and your face has a tendency to be oily (or your bangs or strands along your face are oily because of contact with your makeup), it's possible that only your bangs and the strands of hair along your face need washing. Wash your bangs with a wet washcloth using only a tiny dab of shampoo. Rinse them thoroughly. Apply a conditioner only if your hair is thin and you need it for control.

Beauty Treatment # 3: Condition It

In most cases you want to add a conditioner to your hair after shampooing. However, if you have problems with acne, you should be aware that conditioners can cause or aggravate breakouts. This is because it rubs off on your pillowcase and then gets on your face while you sleep. So if you are acne prone, you may want to skip conditioning. (If you are unsure what to do or you have other questions, ask a dermatologist.) Conditioners smoothes the hair and makes it easier to comb so that it doesn't break off while brushing. It also provides added protection against blow-drying and hot rollers, as well as protection from the elements, such as the sun.

If you look closely at conditioning hair-care products, you will notice that some are called "creme rinse" while others are labeled "conditioner." Both smooth and soften the hair and make it more manageable. The basic difference between a creme rinse and a conditioner is this:

▶ Creme rinse will provide a *light conditioning,* add shine and also detangle the hair so it is easier to brush while wet.

▶ A conditioner is more concentrated than creme rinse and is also more penetrating. Conditioners relax the hair to make it softer and more manageable and give it shine.

Almost all conditioners require that you rinse your hair thoroughly after you've left them on your hair for three to ten minutes. Others are to be left on your hair and do not require that you rinse them out. If your hair is very dry, I would suggest that you look for a conditioner to leave in your hair (especially if you swim in chlorinated pools). Doing this can give you extra protection from the elements.

How to Select a Conditioner

A conditioner, like shampoo, should be selected according to your hair type, such as whether your hair is normal, dry or oily. You especially need to condition your hair if it is naturally dry or dried out due to overexposure from sun, the cold or from swimming in chlorinated pools. After restoring moisture to your hair, you can go for the pizzazz: the conditioner advertising "adds body," "adds shine," or "for limp hair," "for fine hair," and so on.

Experiment with the products until you find those that work for you.

Beauty Treatment # 4: Go Easy on Blow-Dryer

Blow-dryers, hot rollers and crimping and curling irons can dry your hair, as well as can cause split ends, and make your hair brittle, even break off. This is true for blow-drying your hair, especially if you do it often and use dryers higher than 1,400 or 1,600 watts. Almost all of the girls I know own a metal core brush to speed up the drying of their hair. If you do this, use it only when you have to, like at those times when you are running late and need to get going. But don't use it on a daily basis.

Here are some tips to avoid ruining your hair:

▶ Try using a low setting on your dryer, and always use a diffuser (a gadget that attaches to the hairdryer and spreads the air with less force) so the heat damage to the hair is minimized.

▶ When possible, let your hair dry naturally, particularly on the weekends or whenever you have the time to let it dry naturally.

▶ If you're looking for more volume in hair, a vent brush will help; for extra lift, hold your head upside down while you're blow-drying it.

Beauty Treatment # 5: Then and Wow! Choose a Hairstyle That is Right for You

Your hairstyle can dramatically change the way you look. Sometimes it's difficult to tell what you would look like with a certain style. There are two ways to check out how you would look before going and getting a cut, getting a new style, or eyen adding streaks or coloring. First, you can try a wig on before taking any big step. When you do this, use a full-length mirror to analyze the prospective new look from every angle so you can better judge the proportion of your hair to your individual shape. Another way to test a style is to call a salon that uses a video-imaging system to superimpose your face on different hairstyles and in different colors. Some salons will do this as a complimentary service they offer; others may charge a fee.

Video-imaging is a great idea because in addition to seeing what style and what length of hair looks best on you, you can also see what you would look like with black hair or as a brunette, a redhead or blonde. If a picture is worth a thousand words, it might also save you the expense (and heartache) of a haircut (or coloring) that, in the long-run, is not really right for you.

The most important consideration in choosing a hairstyle is that it flatter your features—and, of course, that you like it. Here are some other suggestions for finding a style that's right for you:

- Start by looking around at other people's hair. Look around and notice the styles others are wearing.

- When you see someone with a style you like, observe the person for a moment. Does the style look and "feel" like one you could wear? I remember seeing a woman with a style that I thought was really cool. It was a wedge over one eye, and then I realized the woman had to keep swinging her head from side to side to remove the hair from her eyes. After several moments of observing the woman, I knew for certain that the same hairstyle on me would drive me positively crazy.

- Spend some time looking through magazines seeing the different possibilities, seeing what you like. Could you see yourself wearing any of them? You might even ask your friends if they think a certain style would look good on you.

- Get a professional's opinion. Make an appointment specifically to get advice. Ask a hairstylist what style he or she would suggest, and why.

Does Your Hairstyle Flatter Your Features?

The hairstyle you choose should take into consideration the size and shape of your face and features. Michelle complained that her forehead was too high, but you would never know it because she wore bangs that flattered this feature.

Isn't it nice we girls have so many options with our hair! Like Michelle, who wore her hair in a style that flattered her best features, the right hairstyle can help you play down those things you don't like and accentuate your more flattering features. The following are just a few of the many suggestions I got from a salon owner and popular stylist in my town.

▶ **Your jaw is square.** You can flatter it with a hairstyle that is swept back at the temples. This can be either a short cut that feathers down the neck, or a longer cut that is angled and ends below your chin.

▶ **Your forehead is narrow.** Backcomb the top to make your forehead appear wider.

▶ **Your forehead is really high.** You can fill it in with either a few wisps or bangs or full bangs, or an off-center part with some of your hair falling across the side of your forehead.

▶ **Your neck is short.** A short haircut will create the illusion of a longer neck. Highlights in your hair can draw attention to the hair and not the neck. No bangs.

▶ **Your chin is long.** You can balance it with a haircut that ends at your chin and is rounded and full.

▶ **Your chin is small.** You can enhance it with a hairstyle that ends either above or well below chin length, while also being cut to give you height at the crown.

The important thing is that you have well-groomed hair, and that you really like the way it looks on you.

Beauty Treatment # 6: Scissor Sizzle—Get a Great Haircut

It's probably not wise to trust your haircut to a best friend, brother or younger sister, and you know what happens when your mom says she'll snip "only the dead ends." It's about as disastrous as when you trim it yourself. My suggestion is save up your money and let a professional do it for you. How do you find a good stylist? Referral is always a good place to start. Also, if someone has a hairstyle that you just love, whether it's someone you know or not, it's okay to ask her where she got it done. It's a compliment; most people won't mind your asking.

Here are helpful hints on how to get a good haircut:

- **Do your homework before you walk into the hair salon.** Have an idea of what style you want. Bring a picture of the hairstyle with you or a composite of a couple of styles you like (such as the bangs on one model and the length of hair on another).

- **This is not the time to be shy.** Explain exactly how you would like your hair. Ask the stylist if you are making yourself clear. Don't assume that you are. Kindly ask if he or she would discuss with you his or her opinion as to whether or not it's a style for you.

- **At your appointment say, "Please, no surprises."** Agree beforehand on exactly the length you want and watch carefully. There's nothing worse than a hairstyle or a cut that is not what you want. Pay close attention to what the stylist is doing so that you can tell him or her not to go any shorter, or take off a little more. Some people complain after they've left the salon, but say nothing while their hair is being cut. Don't let this happen to you. It's your hair and if you feel like most people, your hair a large part of your identity.

- **Hold still while your bangs are being cut.** Stylists say it's even wise not to smile while your bangs are being cut because you raise your forehead and it makes the bangs come out shorter than you want them. So sit up straight, and during the time your bangs are being cut, hold your smile.

- **Observe how your stylist is styling your hair** (rather than reading a magazine or listening in on conversation going on in the chair beside you). Ask the stylist why he or she is using a particular size or style of brush, styling with a certain styling product or hair spray, and so on.

- **After you've had a cut or style, ask how to maintain your new style,** or how to brush and dry your hair so it falls in place the way you want it to. Also ask the stylist to suggest the best comb, brush and hair-care products to maintain your new style.

- **Ask questions about your hair.** For example, if you have a cowlick and are unable to tame it by blow-drying it in the opposite direction it grows, ask your hairdresser to apply a perm solution to the roots that will keep it in check. Ask about how to cure frizzy hair, control hair static other than by using hairspray before you brush it, and other things you would like him or her to help troubleshoot.

Beauty Treatment # 7: Color Clarity—Highlighting and Coloring Your Hair

If you are going to color your hair—whether to just a shade darker or lighter than your natural color, or wanting to try chartreuse or lime-green, my suggestion is, don't do it yourself. Every day I see those who have done their own coloring, and usually it's a disaster. Save up your money and have a professional do it. You can really damage your hair if you don't consider the condition your hair is in, and how it will respond to the chemicals in the coloring you're adding. Getting your hair colored in a salon is expensive, but if you shop around and compare, you're sure to find a salon that can do it for you and keep within your budget.

If going all the way with color is too much for you or if your parents are dead set against it, you might try highlighting your hair. Highlights are always a nice touch, and give you an entirely new fresh look. Here are a few good rules to keep in mind before you do:

- Adding a few subtle highlights to the hair on the sides of your face and your bangs can brighten your complexion.
- If you have brown or dark-blonde hair, for a soft and natural look choose amber or gold streaks.
- If your hair is auburn, for a soft and natural look, choose strawberry or gold streaks.
- Never put highlights too closely together or they won't look natural.
- When you apply highlights, if you brush along the curve of the cut, your hair will look fuller and thicker.
- Once you've colored, avoid hot oil treatments because hot oils strip color. Do, however, use a conditioner on a regular basis.

Can You Make Your Hair Grow Faster?

No, you can't, unfortunately. I've checked with the experts and there are simply no reliable products that act as a "fertilizer" to make our hair grow. This is because the part of your hair that you see (the *shaft*) is a nonliving entity (it's made up of keratin). The part responsible for hair growth is the live cells that are deep within the root. At the root level, a hair shaft is created and starts its journey toward becoming your mane.

The process for hair growth is relatively predetermined. Your hair grows in cycles, known as the growing, resting and falling out phase. The *growing phase* is roughly two to five years for healthy hair. During his phase, fresh keratin is released from the root into the strand of hair and this keeps it growing (1/2 inch to 1 inch per month is the norm). The growing phase is followed by a *resting phase*, believed to be only a three- to four-week cycle, before the falling out phase begins. The *falling out phase* lasts somewhere between two and five months, during which time a single strand of hair sheds and is replaced by a new one from the same hair follicle.

Luckily, each hair follicle is independent of the others, each one having their own little calendar to adhere to. This way, we don't shed all of our hair at one time—or else there would be remittent periods when we would each be bald!

But even if you can't make your hair grow faster than it does, there are ways to care for it so it doesn't get overly dry and brittle and break off easily (such as protecting it from the damaging effects of the sun, hair dryers and harsh products).

Wigging Out: Ways to Change Your Style

Hair extensions are really costly, but for special occasions, they can be a great way to add intrigue and pizzazz to your look. The application of hair extensions is very specialized: Every salon doesn't offer them and every hairstylist doesn't have the training to apply them. So, you'll have to find a salon that's equipped to offer hair extensions. They're very expensive, but most likely, you'd be getting them for a special photo or special occasion. Again, ask around, explain exactly what you want and get an estimate of the charges before you schedule an appointment.

You can also wear a wig. Women have been wearing wigs for years, and while I don't suggest you wear a wig all day long, some wigs are lightweight, allow your head to breathe, and look like a real head of hair and not a "wig." I especially like former model and now clothing- and wig-designer, Cheryl Tiegs's line of wigs. My natural hair is auburn brown and I like to wear it long and straight, so I purchased a shorter styled wig. I don't wear the wig very often, but when I do, I really like the way it looks and feels. Prices vary according to whether the wig is made of human hair or synthetic hair.

Because I love to wear my hair long, for me, a short wig is a nice alternative, one that I didn't think I'd try but now that I have, I really like. You may, too, especially if your hair is very slow-growing and there are times you want longer hair, or want to wear a style that is completely different in color or length than your own.

So there you have it—many many things you can do to have simply beautiful hair!

Other Books by Bettie Youngs Book Publishers

Confidence & Self-Esteem for Teens

Jennifer L. Youngs

Confidence & Self-Esteem for Teens is about the ways that beauty manifests from within. Have you ever run across someone who looked pretty, but undid her beauty by the way she acted or treated others?

Compare that to someone who is thoughtful, confident and comfortable with herself and as a result, has a lovely presence about her.

This book shows you how to let your inner beauty shine through—things like the secrets of serenity, steps for staying cool under pressure, building your self-esteem, drawing security from loving others, setting goals and feeling purposeful—and more.

ISBN: 978-1-940784-35-9 • ePub: 978-1-940784-34-2

Health & Fitness for Teens

Jennifer L. Youngs

Health & Fitness for Teens covers a most essential topic for teens: having a healthy body, liking your body and being fit. It's also a time of constant change. We can feel like we're just getting to know who we are when suddenly we are someone totally different. This book uncovers some of the myths teens have for comparing themselves to a standard other than their own, and covers some very important ground on how to best take care of themselves so as to look and feel their very best.

ISBN: 978-1-940784-33-5• ePub: 978-1-940784-32-8

Clothes, Colors and Accessories that Look BEST on YOU: A Guide for Young Adults

Jennifer Leigh Youngs

This fun and fact-filled book shows the teen and young adult how to select clothes, colors and accessories that look best on her; why a certain color makes her feel and look better than others; how to choose a perfume that is the right scent for her skin and chemistry profile; and, provides charts and checklists for being a smart and savvy shopper with all this in mind.

ISBN: 978-1-940784-42-7 • ePub:978-1-940784-43-4

Law of Attraction for Teens

How to Get More of the Good Stuff, and Get Rid of the Bad Stuff!

Christopher Combates

Whether it's getting better grades, creating better relationships, getting into college, or attracting a special someone, the Law of Attraction works! Aligning goals with your intentions enables you to create a better life. Written for teens, this engaging book will help teens to set purposeful goals, and to think, act, andcommunicate in the most positive way possible.

ISBN: 978-1-936332-29-8• ePub: 978-1-936332-30-4

Lessons from the Gym For Young Adults

5 Secrets for Being in Control of Your Life

Chris Cucchiara

As a teen, Chris Cucchiara's life was a mess. Then he discovered the gym and he was transformed inside and out. Says Chris, "The gym taught me discipline, which led to achieving goals, which started a cycle of success." A much-admired high-performance coach for teens, in this book, Chris share his guiding principles on how to: develop mental toughness (a life without fear, stress, and anger); become and stay healthy and fit; build an "athlete for life" mentality that stresses excellence; and, set and achieve goals that matter.

ISBN: 978-1-936332-38-0 • ePub: 978-1-936332-34-2

Lessons from the Gym For Young Adults

Workbook

Chris Cucchiara

A SUCCESS WORKBOOK FOR YOUNG ADULTS (ages 12-20) Do you lack self-confidence or have a difficult time making decisions? Do you sometimes wonder what is worth doing? Do you ever have a tough time feeling a sense of purpose and belonging? Chris shares his expertise of mastering success principles and shows you how to: Discover your real passion and purpose in life, which provides the drive, ambition and determination to overcome your limiting beliefs, fears, stress, and anger; Feel more in control of your life; Build your confidence and self-esteem; Build an athlete for life mentality that stresses leadership and excellence as a mindset; and, Stay motivated and set and achieve goals.

ISBN: 978-1-940784-16-8

GPS YOUR BEST LIFE

Charting Your Destination and Getting There in Style

Charmaine Hammond and Debra Kasowski
Foreword by Jack Canfield

A most useful guide to charting and traversing the many options that lay before you.

"A perfect book for servicing your most important vehicle: yourself. No matter where you are in your life, the concepts and direction provided in this book will help you get to a better place. It's a must read." **—Ken Kragen, author of *Life Is a Contact Sport*, and organizer of *We Are the World*, and *Hands Across America*, and other historic humanitarian events**

ISBN: 978-1-936332-26-7 • ePub: 978-1-936332-41-0

News Girls Don't Cry

Melissa McCarty

Today the host of ORA TV's Newsbreaker, and now calling Larry King her boss, Melissa McCarty worked her way up through the trenches of live television news. But she was also running away from her past, one of growing up in the roughest of neighborhoods, watching so many she knew—including her brother—succumb to drugs, gangs, and violence. It was a past that forced her to be tough and streetwise, traits that in her career as a popular television newscaster, would end up working against her.

Every tragic story she covered was a grim reminder of where she'd been. But the practiced and restrained emotion given to the camera became her protective armor even in her private life where she was unable to let her guard down—a demeanor that damaged both her personal and professional relationships. In News Girls Don't Cry, McCarty confronts the memory-demons of her past, exploring how they hardened her—and how she turned it all around.

An inspiring story of overcoming adversity, welcoming second chances, and becoming happy and authentic.

"A battle between personal success and private anguish, a captivating brave tale of a woman's drive to succed and her tireless struggle to keep her family intact. The reader is pulled into Melissa's story… an honest account of the common battle of addiction." **—Susan Hendricks, CNN Headline News Anchor**

ISBN: 978-1-936332-69-4 • ePub: 978-1-936332-70-0

The Predatory Lies of Anorexia
A Survivor's Story

Abby D. Kelly

"I want...I want you to think I am the smartest, the thinnest, the most beautiful..."

With these words, Abby Kelly encapsulates the overwhelming struggle of her 15-year bout with anorexia. Abby lays bare the reality of anorexia, beginning in her teenage years, when the predatory lies of the disease took root in her psyche as she felt pressured from family and peers for not being "enough." In her quest for a greater sense of personal power, she concludes "I'll be 'more', but it will be on my terms."

Her reasoning is a classic example as to why and how eating disorders dig in and persist as long as they do.

From this new self-awareness, Abby targets her body as the agent to show others that she is disciplined and focused. She sets out to restrict her food intake and adheres to an extreme schedule of exercise. While others close to Abby see a person who is dangerously thin, Abby, in fact, derives a sense of personal achievement from her weight loss.

Abby exposes the battles, defeats, and ultimate triumph—taking the reader on a poignant odyssey from onset to recovery, including how she set out to fool the many who tried to help her, from dietitians to therapists, from one inpatient treatment center after another, and reveals not only the victim's suffering, but that of those who love her.

This raw and passionate story eloquently describes how Abby finally freed herself from this life-threatening condition, and how others can find courage and hope for recovery, too.

"This beautifully written book paints an exacting picture of Anorexia, one that is sure to help legions of those suffering from this most serious and life-threatening condition."
—Amy Dardis, founder and editor of Haven Journal

ISBN: 978-1-940784-17-5 • ePub: 978-1-940784-18-2

Electric Living
The Science behind the Law of Attraction

Kolie Crutcher

An electrical engineer by training, Crutcher applies his in-depth knowledge of electrical engineering principles and practical engineering experience detailing the scientific explanation of why human beings become what they think. A practical, step-by-step guide to help you harness your thoughts and emotions so that the Law of Attraction will benefit you.

ISBN: 978-1-936332-58-8 • ePub: 978-1-936332-59-5

The Aspiring Actor's Handbook

Molly Cheek and Debbie Zip

Concise and straightforward, The Aspiring Actor's Handbook is written for curious and aspiring actors to help them make informed decisions while pursuing this exciting career.

Veteran actresses Molly Cheek and Debbie Zipp have culled the wit and wisdom of a wide array of successful actors, from Beth Grant to Dee Wallace, and collected the kind of mentoring perspective so many in the business wish they'd had when they were just starting out. Get insider information and real-life experiences and personal stories that range from how to get your foot in the door to becoming a career actor. Get the inside scoop from successful veteran actors on how to work with agents and unions; manage finances; prepare for auditions; cope with rejection—and success—and much more.

ISBN: 978-1-940784-12-0 • ePub: 978-1-940784-02-1

Fastest Man in the World
The Tony Volpentest Story

Tony Volpentest
Foreword by Ross Perot

Tony Volpentest, a four-time Paralympic gold medalist and five-time world champion sprinter, is a 2012 nominee for the Olympic Hall of Fame. This inspirational story details his being born without feet, to holding records as the fastest sprinter in the world.

"This inspiring story is about the thrill of victory to be sure—winning gold—but it is also a reminder about human potential: the willingness to push ourselves beyond the ledge of our own imagination. A powerfully inspirational story." **—Charlie Huebner, United States Olympic Committee**

ISBN: 978-1-940784-07-6 • ePub: 978-1-940784-08-3

On Toby's Terms

Charmaine Hammond

On Toby's Terms is an endearing story of a beguiling creature who teaches his owners that, despite their trying to teach him how to be the dog they want, he is the one to lay out the terms of being the dog he needs to be. This insight would change their lives forever.

"This is a captivating, heartwarming story and we are very excited about bringing it to film." **—Steve Hudis, Producer**

ISBN: 978-0-9843081-4-9 • ePub: 978-1-936332-15-1

The Story of Millard and Linda Fuller, Founders of Habitat for Humanity and The Fuller Center for Housing

Bettie B. Youngs

Everyone has heard of Habitat for Humanity, the faith-based housing initiative that has built homes for more than a million of the world's poor. Many are familiar with its founders, Millard and Linda Fuller. But few know the amazing love story behind the movement—a story that began accidentally and will conclude in a world forever changed by its impact.

By age 29, Millard Fuller was a self-made millionaire. But that success came at a cost. He never took a family vacation, had kids he barely knew, and a lonely wife who was about to leave him. Ultimately, realizing that he was about to lose what really mattered, Fuller reconciled with his wife and rearranged his priorities.

In 1965, the Fullers gave away their personal fortune and dedicated their lives to serving others, eventually founding Habitat for Humanity in 1976. In this capacity, the Fullers traveled the globe, receiving the praise of prime ministers and presidents, sharing meals with prisoners, and appealing for funds and volunteers. More important than any accolade or award were the homes they built and the hope they gave. The Fullers have done more for the cause of housing the poor than any other couple in history.

Eventually, a struggle for the reins of the most beloved nonprofit of our times would result in the firing of Millard and Linda by Habitat International's board of directors. This certainly didn't mean the end to their vision—the Fullers would rebound, continuing to support local Habitat affiliates and beginning The Fuller Center for Housing, determined to pursue their dream of building for people everywhere simple, decent places to live.

ISBN: 978-0-9882848-8-3 • ePub: 978-1-936332-53-3

The Girl Who Gave Her Wish Away

Sharon Babineau
Foreword by Craig Kielburger

The Children's Wish Foundation approached lovely thirteen-year-old Maddison Babineau just after she received her cancer diagnosis. "You can have anything," they told her, "a Disney cruise? The chance to meet your favorite movie star? A five thousand dollar shopping spree?"

Maddie knew exactly what she wanted. She had recently been moved to tears after watching a television program about the plight of orphaned children. Maddie's wish? To ease the suffering of these children half-way across the world. Despite the ravishing cancer, she became an indefatigable fundraiser for "her children." In The Girl Who Gave Wish Away, her mother reveals Maddie's remarkable journey of providing hope and future to the village children who had filled her heart.

A special story, heartwarming and reassuring.

ISBN: 978-1-936332-96-0 • ePub: 978-1-936332-97-7

Karmic Alibi

Gaining EXPEDIENT Wisdom by Leaving Your Excuses Behind

Patricia Karen Gagic

Karma is a potent law of the universe. Karma, literally meaning "action," is the sum of your intentional and deliberate consciousness, which prescribes your thoughts and thus determines your actions.

Just as positive thoughts initiate positive outcomes, negative thoughts create angst. The "wisdom" of your Karma is yours alone; you cannot experience someone else's Karma.

In Karmic Alibi, expert Patricia Gagic shares how you can influence the sovereignty of your Karma. By mastering the "five radical degrees of life" you can expedite the wisdom of your Karma so as to live in a state of joyful and purpose-filled abundance emotionally, physically and spiritually—which is your divine right.

In this soulful and most insightful book, Patricia examines her own beliefs and describes how she transformed them. By using examples from her life, and thanks to the trail markers she leaves along the way, she makes it easier for each of us to create the life we wish to live, too.

ISBN: 978-1-940784-29-8 • ePub: 978-1-940784-30-4

Healthy Family, Happy Life

What Healthy Families Learn from Healthy Moms

Donna Schuller

Family, Health, Fitness & Nutrition expert Donna Schuller offers advice for improving health and wellness including the benefits the and paybacks of being honest with others; how wellness thoughts contribute to your being healthy; the significance of loving others and the imperative of loving oneself of exercise, sleep and happiness; how to get through hard times; how dietary supplementation work; the importance of nutrition, and more.

ISBN: 978-1-940784-11-3 • ePub: 978-1-940784-31-1

Red Dot

An Inspirational Short Story about a Remarkable Dog and the Children He Loved

Bettie J. Burres

Nothing compares to the faithfulness of the family dog. For six years Teddy has helped out on the family farm, walked the kids to the school bus, comforted them when they were sad, and snuggled with them through cold winter nights. In the dusk of a warm summer evening, when an intruder makes his way through the yard, threatening all that Teddy holds dear, the four children learn a devastating truth about the meaning of faithfulness.

A touching story of love—and ultimately, forgiveness.

ISBN: 978-1-936332-66-3• ePub: 978-1-936332-73-1

Last Reader Standing
. . . The Story of a Man Who Learned to Read at 54

Archie Willard
with Colleen Wiemerslage

The day Archie lost his thirty-one year job as a laborer at a meat packing company, he was forced to confront the secret he had held so closely for most of his life: at the age of fifty-four, he couldn't read. For all his adult life, he'd been able to skirt around the issue. But now, forced to find a new job to support his family, he could no longer hide from the truth.

Last Reader Standing is the story of Archie's amazing—and often painful—journey of becoming literate at middle age, struggling with the newfound knowledge of his dyslexia. From the little boy who was banished to the back of the classroom because the teachers labeled him "stupid," Archie emerged to becoming a national figure who continues to enlighten professionals into the world of the learning disabled. He joined Barbara Bush on stage for her Literacy Foundation's fundraisers where she proudly introduced him as "the man who took advantage of a second chance and improved his life."

This is a touching and poignant story that gives us an eye-opening view of the lack of literacy in our society, and how important it is for all of us to have opportunity to become all that we can be—to have hope and go after our dreams.

At the age of eighty-two, Archie continues to work with literacy issues in medicine and consumerism.

> "Archie . . . you need to continue spreading the word." —**Barbara Bush, founder of the Literacy Foundation, and First Lady and wife of George H. W. Bush, the 41st President of the United States**

ISBN: 978-1-936332-48-9 • ePub: 978-1-936332-50-2

Abuconodozor
A Cat with An Attitude

John Rixey Moore

A darling and memorable cat story about a "not at-all-a-cat-person" who comes home one day to find that a stray Abssinian cat has decided to take up residency in his home. Reluctantly, he feeds the cat, and allows the cat to sleep on his bed. He begins to adore the cat, and comes to admire and respect her regal qualities, eventually naming the cat for an Abyssinian pharaoh, Abucodonozor. But the cat has a different idea.

ISBN: 978-1-940784-13-7 • ePub: 978-1-936332-89-2

FOR MORE READING
VISIT OUR WEBSITE AT:
www.BettieYoungsBooks.com

CPSIA information can be obtained
at www.ICGtesting.com
Printed in the USA
FSHW010900150121
77589FS

9 781940 784441